Fanny Jackson Coppin

REMINISCENCES OF SCHOOL LIFE, AND HINTS ON TEACHING

AFRICAN-AMERICAN WOMEN WRITERS, 1910–1940

HENRY LOUIS GATES, JR. *General Editor*

Jennifer Burton *Associate Editor*

FANNY JACKSON COPPIN

REMINISCENCES OF SCHOOL LIFE, AND HINTS ON TEACHING

Introduction by
SHELLEY P. HALEY

G.K. HALL & CO.
An Imprint of Simon & Schuster Macmillan
New York

Prentice Hall International
London   Mexico City   New Delhi   Singapore   Sydney   Toronto

G.K. Hall & Co.
An Imprint of Simon & Schuster Macmillan
866 Third Avenue
New York, NY 10022

Library of Congress Catalog Card Number: 94-19855

Printed in the United States of America

Printing Number
1 2 3 4 5 6 7 8 9 10

Library of Congress Cataloging-in-Publication Data
The Library of Congress has catralogued the hardcover edition of this book as follows:

Coppin, Fanny Jackson.
Reminiscences of school life and hints on teaching / Frances Jackson Coppin ; introduction by Shelley P. Haley.
p. cm.— (African American women writers, 1910–1940)
Originally published: Philadelphia : African Methodist Episcopal Book Concern, 1913. With new introd.
Includes bibliographical references.
ISBN 0-8161-1633-4 (alk. paper)
1. Coppin, Fanny Jackson. 2. Institute for Colored Youth (Philadelphia, Pa.)—History. 3. Teachers—Pennsylvania—Philadelphia—Biography. 4. Education—Philosophy. 5. Teaching. I. Title. II. Series.
LD7501.P495C67 1994
370'.92—dc20
[B]
                                                                94-19855
                                                                CIP

ISBN (hardcover) 0-8161-1633-4
ISBN (paperback) 0-7838-1396-1

This paper meets the requirements of ANSI/NISO Z39.48-1992 (Permanence of Paper).

C O N T E N T S

GENERAL EDITORS' PREFACE

The past decade of our literary history might be thought of as the era of African-American women writers. Culminating in the awarding of the Pulitzer Prize to Toni Morrison and Rita Dove and the Nobel Prize for Literature to Toni Morrison in 1993, and characterized by the presence of several writers—Toni Morrison, Alice Walker, Maya Angelou, and the Delany Sisters, among others—on the *New York Times* Best Seller List, the shape of the most recent period in our literary history has been determined in large part by the writings of black women.

This, of course, has not always been the case. African-American women authors have been publishing their thoughts and feelings at least since 1773, when Phillis Wheatley published her book of poems in London, thereby bringing poetry directly to bear upon the philosophical discourse over the African's "place in nature" and his or her place in the great chain of being. The scores of words published by black women in America in the nineteenth century—most of which were published in extremely limited editions and never reprinted—have been republished in new critical editions in the forty-volume *Schomburg Library of Nineteenth-Century Black Women Writers*. The critical response to that series has led to requests from scholars and students alike for a similar series, one geared to the work by black women published between 1910 and the beginning of World War Two.

African-American Women Writers, 1910–1940 is designed to bring back into print many writers who otherwise would be unknown to contemporary readers, and to increase the availability of lesser-known texts by established writers who originally published during this critical period in African-American letters. This series implicitly acts as a chronological sequel to the Schomburg series, which focused on the origins of the black female literary tradition in America.

In less than a decade, the study of African-American women's writings has grown from its promising beginnings into a firmly established field in departments of English, American Studies, and African-American Studies. A comparison of the form and function of the original series and this sequel illustrates this dramatic shift. The *Schomburg Library* was published at the cusp of focused academic investigation into the interplay between race and gender. It covered the extensive period from the publication of Phillis Wheatley's *Poems on Various Subjects, Religious and Moral* in 1773 through the "Black Women's Era" of 1890–1910, and was designed to be an inclusive series of the major early texts by black women writers. The Schomburg Library provided a historical backdrop for black women's writings of the 1970s and 1980s, including the works of writers such as Toni Morrison, Alice Walker, Maya Angelou, and Rita Dove.

African-American Women Writers, 1910–1940 continues our effort to provide a new generation of readers access to texts—historical, sociological, and literary—that have been largely "unread" for most of this century. The series bypasses works that are important both to the period and the tradition, but that are readily available, such as Zora Neale Hurston's *Their Eyes Were Watching God*, Jessie Fauset's *Plum Bun* and *There is Confusion*, and Nella Larsen's *Quicksand* and *Passing*. Our goal is to provide access to a wide variety of rare texts. The series includes Fauset's two other novels, *The Chinaberry Tree: A Novel of American Life* and *Comedy: American Style*, and Hurston's short play, *Color Struck*, since these are not yet widely available. It also features works by virtually unknown writers, such as *A Tiny Spark*, Christina Moody's slim volume of poetry self-published in 1910, and *Reminiscences of School Life, and Hints on Teaching*, written by Fanny Jackson Coppin in the last year of her life (1913), a multigenre work combining an autobiographical sketch and reflections on trips to England and South Africa, complete with pedagogical advice.

Cultural studies' investment in diverse resources allows the historic scope of the *African-American Women Writers* series to be more focused than the *Schomburg Library* series, which covered works written over a 137-year period. With few exceptions, the authors included in the *African-American Women Writers* series wrote their major works between 1910 and 1940. The texts reprinted include all of the works by each particular author that are not otherwise readily obtainable. As a result, two volumes contain works originally published after 1940. The Charlotte Hawkins Brown volume includes her book of etiquette published in 1941, *The Correct Thing To Do—To Say—To Wear*. One of the poetry volumes contains Maggie Pogue Johnson's *Fallen Blossoms*, published in 1951, a compilation of all her previously published and unpublished poems.

Excavational work by scholars during the past decade has been crucial to the development of *African-American Women Writers, 1910–1940*. Germinal bibliographic sources such as Anne Allen Shockley's *Afro-American Women Writers 1746–1933* and Maryemma Graham's *Database of African-American Women Writers* made the initial identification of texts possible. Other works were brought to our attention by scholars who wrote letters sharing their research. Additional texts by selected authors were then added, so that many volumes contain the complete oeuvres of particular writers. Pieces by authors without enough published work to fill an entire volume were grouped with other pieces by genre.

The two types of collections, those organized by author and those organized by genre, bring out different characteristics of black women's writings of the period. The collected works of the literary writers illustrate that many of them were experimenting with a variety of forms. Mercedes Gilbert's volume, for example, contains her 1931 collection, *Selected Gems of Poetry, Comedy, and Drama, Etc.*, as well as her 1938 novel, *Aunt Sara's Wooden God*. Georgia Douglas Johnson's volume contains her plays and short stories in addition to her poetry. Sarah Lee Brown Fleming's volume combines her 1918 novel *Hope's Highway* with her 1920 collection of poetry, *Clouds and Sunshine*.

The generic volumes both bring out the formal and thematic similarities among many of the writings and highlight the striking individuality of particular writers. Most of the plays in the volume of one-acts are social dramas whose tragic endings can be clearly attributed to miscegenation and racism. Within the context of these other plays, Marita Bonner's surrealistic theatrical vision becomes all the more striking.

The volumes of *African-American Women Writers, 1910–1940* contain reproductions of more than one hundred previously published texts, including twenty-nine plays, seventeen poetry collections, twelve novels, six autobiographies, five collections of short biographical sketches, three biographies, three histories of organizations, three black histories, two anthologies, two sociological studies, a diary, and a book of etiquette. Each volume features an introduction written by a contemporary scholar that provides crucial biographical data on each author and the historical and critical context of her work. In some cases, little information on the authors was available outside of the fragments of biographical data contained in the original introduction or in the text itself. In these instances, editors have documented the libraries and research centers where they tried to find information, in the hope that subsequent scholars will continue the necessary search to find the "lost" clues to the women's stories in the rich stores of papers, letters, photographs, and other primary materials scattered throughout the country that have yet to be fully catalogued.

Many of the thrilling moments that occurred during the development of this series were the result of previously fragmented pieces of these women's histories suddenly coming together, such as Adele Alexander's uncovering of an old family photograph, picturing her own aunt with Addie Hunton, the author Alexander was researching. Claudia Tate's examination of Georgia Douglas Johnson's papers in the Moorland-Spingarn Research Center of Howard University resulted in the discovery of a wealth of previously unpublished work.

The slippery quality of race itself emerged during the construction of the series. One of the short novels originally intended for inclusion in the series had to be cut when the family of the author protested that the writer was not of African descent. Another case involved Louise Kennedy's sociological study *The Negro Peasant Turns Inward*. The fact that none of the available biographical material on Kennedy specifically mentioned race, combined with some coded criticism in a review in the *Crisis*, convinced editor Sheila Smith McCoy that Kennedy was probably white.

These women, taken together, begin to chart the true vitality, and complexity, of the literary tradition that African-American women have generated, using a wide variety of forms. They testify to the fact that the monumental works of Hurston, Larsen, and Fauset, for example, emerged out of a larger cultural context; they were not exceptions or aberrations. Indeed, their contributions to American literature and culture, as this series makes clear, were fundamental not only to the shaping of the African-American tradition but to the American tradition as well.

Henry Louis Gates, Jr.
Jennifer Burton

PUBLISHER'S NOTE

In the *African-American Women Writers, 1910-1940* series, G.K. Hall not only is making available previously neglected works that, in many cases, have been long out of print; we are also, whenever possible, publishing these works in facsimiles reprinted from their original editions including, when available, reproductions of original title pages, copyright pages, and photographs.

When it was not possible for us to reproduce a complete facsimile edition of a particular work (for example, if the original exists only as a handwritten draft or is too fragile to be reproduced), we have attempted to preserve the essence of the original by resetting the work exactly as it originally appeared. Therefore, any typographical errors, strikeouts, or other anomalies reflect our efforts to give the reader a true sense of the original work.

We trust that these facsimile and reprint editions, together with the new introductory essays, will be both useful and historically enlightening to scholars and students alike.

INTRODUCTION

BY SHELLEY P. HALEY

Fannie Barrier Williams paid the following tribute to Fanny M. Jackson Coppin:

> By common consent Mrs. Fannie [*sic*] Jackson Coppin ranks first in mental equipment, in natural gifts and achievements among colored teachers. She was among the first colored women of this country to receive a college education, having graduated from Oberlin. From Oberlin she went to Philadelphia, where for more than thirty years she was principal of the Institution [*sic*] for Colored Youth, and was the most thoroughly controlling influence in moulding the lives and character of the colored people of that great city. Mrs. Coppin would be regarded as eminent in any race where superior worth and dominant influence for the good are recognized and properly rewarded.[1]

This reverent and deferential accolade meant more to Fanny Jackson Coppin than many others that she received because it came from a fellow black woman and sister in the struggle to uphold the dignity of black women. Yet once we explore the passion and dedication Coppin devoted to education, once we consider the gender and racial obstacles placed in her way, Williams's tribute pales before the accomplishments of this woman.

In many different areas, Fanny Jackson Coppin was a foremother and pioneer for many black women, both of her own and later generations. In her journalistic endeavors for the *Christian Recorder*, Coppin foreshadowed Ida B. Wells; in her activism for social and educational reform, Mary Church Terrell; in her championing of vocational training for girls and young women, Nannie Helen Burroughs; and in her practice and expression of black feminism, in her independence of thought, in her pioneer role as a high school principal, in her advocacy of choice in educational curricula, and in her knowledge and love of the classical languages, Coppin was the foremother to Anna Julia Cooper.

Despite these path-breaking contributions in so many fields, Coppin is virtually unknown to journalists, historians of education and classicists. Clearly, the reason is the racism and sexism of American society and more particularly of its microcosm, the American academy. Coppin's invisibility cannot be excused by lack of records of her life or of her work. Documentation of her years as principal of the Institute for Colored Youth (ICY) in Philadelphia, a post she held from 1869 to 1902, survives in the Friends Historical Library at Swarthmore College and in the Quaker records housed at Haverford College. Coppin's newspaper column, "Women's Department," which she wrote for the *Christian Recorder* under the pseudonym Catherine Casey beginning in 1878, is available on microfilm. Coppin's husband, Levi J. Coppin, in his 1919 autobiography *Unwritten History* (an odd title for a printed text), left one of the few accounts of Fanny J. Coppin's personal life. Interestingly, Levi Coppin seems to have taken the title for his autobiography from a lecture of the same name that Fanny J. Coppin delivered to a group of black women in the early 1890s.

The volume reprinted here, *Reminiscences of School Life, and Hints on Teaching*, was written by Fanny Jackson Coppin during the last year of her life (1913), and includes an autobiographical sketch, practical hints from an experienced classroom teacher, and reflections on two journeys, one to England and one to South Africa. The work is, as the title indicates, a series of memories and recollections of Coppin's childhood, the beginning of her educational career, and the launching of her choice-in-education campaign. The last theme refers to Coppin's fervent belief that black students should have a choice in the educational curricula they pursue. She transformed this belief into the establishment of the Industrial Department of ICY. As a result, industrial and vocational training courses coexisted with the traditional classics courses at the school. This choice of curricula was dependent on and only limited by the talents and interests of the student, not the prevailing notions of racial politics or the bigoted perspective of scientific racism.

Reminiscences is an anthology of four parts, rather than a cohesive single volume. The first is an autobiographical sketch that relates remarkably little personal information. Coppin was obviously uncomfortable talking about herself; the tone is self-effacing and unpretentious. Her discomfort is reflected further in her fluctuation between first- and third-person narrative, as when she is describing how she gained her freedom: "Sarah [Coppin's maternal aunt] went to work at six dollars a month, saved one hundred and twenty-five dollars and bought little Frances, having taken a great liking to her, for on account of my birth, my grandfather refused to buy my mother; and so I was left a slave in the District of Columbia where I was born."[2]

The voice in the second part of her work, *Hints on Teaching*, is much more confident and secure. Coppin was an experienced teacher and as such strongly believed that education, especially elementary education, should be child-centered. In her vision the teacher should be, in modern educational jargon, a facilitator of learning, not an obstruction. For instance, her advice on teaching reading and spelling contains this observation: "It is objected that if we leave the corrections until the reading is finished, they will be forgotten; but stopping after each one reads, to say what you noticed is wrong, etc., keeps the pupils from getting a connected idea of the lesson, and hence, destroys the interest in it" (*Reminiscences*, 68).

The third part of the anthology is a travelogue describing Coppin's two international journeys, to England and South Africa. In the essay on her trip to England, Coppin seized the opportunity to voice her feminist stance in regard to the Protestant church hierarchy's division of labor. A Presbyterian minister got Coppin "riled" by attempting to curtail the "ecclesiastical functions" of women (*Reminiscences*, 118). Coppin responded that "it may very well be said of women that while they are and were created second, they were not only created with body, but they were created also with a head, and they are responsible therefore to decide in certain matters and to use their own judgement. It is very true, as I will certainly say, that fools rush in where angels fear to tread; but then I question as to whether all fools are confined to the feminine gender" (*Reminiscences*, 119).

The final part of *Reminiscences* describes Coppin's visit to South Africa, where she had traveled as a missionary with her husband, a minister. It shows Coppin continuing as an educational activist, although in this case the education is religious. She worked with the native women of the Bulawayo mission to establish missionary societies and schools. Like other missionaries of the time, Coppin held a Christian-centered point of view: "They have religious views before we reach them. Crude, of course; unenlightened, uncertain, speculative, false, just as all people hold who have not been give the true word of God" (*Reminiscences*, 129–30). But Coppin, unlike white missionaries, recognized that Africans were a highly moral people: "They already have, as it were, an intuitive sense of right and wrong, hence they do no harm to the stranger in their midst. Indeed, our religious teaching is, in a sense, but an explanation of their own religious impulses" (*Reminiscences*, 130).

In his autobiography, Reverend Coppin remarked upon how pleased the African women were to have "one of their sisters" from America come and help them in their church work. He goes on to observe that "Africa is not unlike other portions of the world in its habit of holding the women back. The coming of Christianity everywhere marks the beginning of woman's emancipation. Christianity in Africa must not mean less."[3] Given Fanny J. Coppin's exchange with the Presbyterian minister in England, she was aware that the hierarchical organization (if not the theology) of Christianity was repressive for women.

Included with *Reminiscences of School Life, and Hints on Teaching* is a gazetteer of the faculty and students who were at the Institute of Colored Youth while Coppin was a teacher and administrator there. Although Coppin assembled the data, it was arranged and written by her friend and admirer W. C. Bolivar, who had been a student at ICY. Bolivar ends his introduction to the second part of the book with this qualification: "This is simply a supplementary pointer to an aftermath of splendid effort, as seen in the first part; and in no sense an introduction—for who is there to introduce a woman like Fanny M. Jackson Coppin?" (*Reminiscences*, 188). The compilation of the achievements of Coppin's students reads like a Who's Who of the black middle and professional classes in Philadelphia and beyond. Coppin touched and changed the lives of all these students with her commitment to student-centered education.

In a 1890 tribute published in the *New York Age* to Fanny J. Coppin on her twenty-fifth anniversary of service to ICY, John Durham, one of her former students, remarks in several places upon Coppin's kindness and modesty.[4] She evaded his request for an interview for some time; ". . . she works on modestly—indeed too self-deprecatingly—eminent but without notoriety." He describes her modesty as "almost aggravating" to her friends, yet at the same time she is "well known as an agitator" (Durham). Coppin herself conveys these same qualities of modesty, simplicity, self-deprecation, and commitment to social and educational reform in the autobiographical sketch of *Reminiscences*. With characteristic altruism, Coppin explains in the book's very first sentence why she finally has agreed to write down her life: "There are some few points in my life which 'some forlorn and shipwrecked brother seeing, may take heart again'" (*Reminiscences*, 9). These "few points," however, serve to whet our curiosity rather than satisfy it. Born into slavery in 1837 in Washington, D.C., Coppin's earliest memory is that of her grandmother's one-room cabin. Her first intellectual puzzle comes at the age of three, when she is intrigued by the word *offspring*. Coppin's grandmother had six children: three boys and three girls. Coppin mentions that her enslaved grandfather, Henry Orr, bought himself and four of his children (his three sons and a daughter Sarah). Coppin also states that her mother Lucy was not bought and freed by her father because of her (Fanny's) birth; mother and daughter remained slaves in the District of Columbia. Sarah Orr, her aunt, worked, saved, and bought Fanny for $125; Fanny was twelve or thirteen at the time. She was grateful to her aunt Sarah and dedicated *Reminiscences* to her. But what feelings did she have for her grandfather and her mother? Henry Orr was a mulatto and free man; he was a prominent waiter and caterer in Washington, D.C.[5] He had purchased freedom for his sons John, William Henry, and Moses when they were ages nine, seven, and five, respectively. However, Orr did not buy Sarah's freedom; she was not free until she was thirty and about to be married. His daughter Rebecca was freed in Orr's will, and Lucy was never freed because of Fanny's birth.[6] Did Coppin feel resentment or bitterness toward her grandfather? Was this the seed that would blossom into Coppin's black feminism? Orr clearly allowed his daughters to remain enslaved to avoid assuming financial responsibility for them (Perkins, 14). He does not seem to have purchased his wife and he never forgave Lucy for the circumstances of Coppin's birth. Unfortunately, Fanny Jackson never mentions exactly what these circumstances were. Was it severe moralism that prompted Orr's actions in refusing to free Lucy? How did Lucy react to this rejection? Did she resent Fanny or abuse her because of it? What kind of relationship did Coppin have with her mother? In her autobiography, Coppin speaks only of the aunts who helped her get positions and an education, beginning with her Aunt Sarah, who freed her. And what of Coppin's father? Can we ever determine who he was? Was he a "senator from Carolina" as Alfred Vance Churchill claimed in 1953?[7] Coppin herself never mentions her father and so we are left with many questions and few answers.

Coppin's early childhood experiences remind us of the dangers of childhood for all children in the nineteenth century. Without laying blame or making accusations, Coppin relates how she received two severe burnings and reflects on the inadequacies of nineteenth-century day-care for children with the simple statement "There were no Day Nurseries then" (*Reminiscences*, 10).

In her quest for education, Coppin encountered more obstacles than dangers. Once legally free, she was determined to be financially independent as well. Coppin was equally determined to get an education to satisfy that intellectual curiosity she had demonstrated at an early age. After obtaining her freedom, Coppin moved to New Bedford, Massachusetts, where her Aunt Rebecca arranged a position for her and where she could begin her education. In a description reminiscent of Cinderella and not without ironic wit, Coppin tells of her first job as a free young black woman: "She [her Aunt Rebecca] put me out to work, at a place where I was allowed to go to school when I was not at work. But I could not go on wash day, nor ironing day, nor cleaning day and this interfered with my progress. There were no Hamptons and no night schools then" (*Reminiscences*, 11).

Sarah Orr had bought Coppin because she had "taken a great liking to her" (*Reminiscences*, 10), but also, I suspect, because she perceived Coppin's intellectual gifts. Although Coppin does not mention it in her autobiographical sketch, her employment in domestic service upset Orr. She may have worried that Coppin would never have the time to fulfill her academic potential, but there was also an element of classism in her anxiety. John W. Cromwell quotes Coppin speaking about this time of her life: "'So I went to service. Oh the hue and cry there was, when I went out to live! Even my aunt spoke of it; she had a home to offer me; but the "slavish" element was so strong in me that I must make myself a servant. Ah, how those things cut me then! But I knew I was right, and I kept straight on. . . .'"[8] As a consequence, Coppin always had the highest respect for women who were in domestic service and for working-class people in general.

Luckily Coppin found another position, this time with the family of George H. Calvert. Coppin enthusiastically relates the genealogy of Calvert, "a great grandson of Lord Baltimore," and his wife Elizabeth Stuart Calvert, "descendant of Mary, Queen of Scots" (*Reminiscences*, 11). Coppin does not make this point because she is a snob, but rather because she associated the Calverts with educated and therefore enlightened people. To her mind education was the tool that removed the ignorance that was at the root of racism and bigotry. She felt it was impossible to be both educated and unenlightened about racism. Moreover, the Calverts represented Coppin's first real opportunity to educate herself. Many literary persons visited the house; she was allowed to hire a tutor from her earnings and she attended the black schools of Newport, Rhode Island. She then prepared to enter the Rhode Island Normal School, and in what reads like a religious conversion, she finds her true calling: "Here, my eyes were first opened to the subject of teaching. I said to myself, is it possible that teaching can be made so interesting as this!" (*Reminiscences*, 11). Later, she relates that, although happy with the Calverts, "it was in me to get an education and teach my people. This idea was deep in my soul. Where it came from I cannot tell, for I never had any exhortations, nor any lectures which influenced me to take this course. It must have been born in me" (*Reminiscences*, 17).

Elizabeth Calvert was upset that Coppin chose to leave her employment. Coppin admits that they were close and Coppin, at least, perceived her position as that of a daughter to Calvert. Yet there are hints that power and not only affection framed this relationship. Indeed, it is clear that the power relationship of mistress and servant was never far from the surface. For example, Coppin took music lessons and never told Calvert; she kept a piano at the house of her aunt Elizabeth Orr (an aunt by marriage). Without informing Calvert, Coppin regularly attended her Wednesday music lessons. Eventually, of course, Calvert noted Coppin's Wednesday absences and when she summoned Coppin for an explanation Coppin clearly expected physical punishment: "I was very much afraid that something quite unpleasant awaited me. . . ." (*Reminiscences*, 16). The question that comes immediately to mind is why Coppin, even with her proclamations of affection, distrusted Calvert to the extent that she could not inform her about the music lessons.

It was important to Coppin to be educated, not only for the public good, but also for her personal well-being. As a teacher, she would be independent; she would be her own person. Coppin had heard of Oberlin, perhaps at Rhode Island State Normal, and she set enrollment there as her major goal. In 1860 she enrolled in the "Ladies Department" to prepare for entrance to the "Collegiate Department." Since, as Coppin observes, "the course of study there [at Oberlin] being the same as that at Harvard" (*Reminiscences*, 12), that is, fundamentally a classical curriculum, Coppin had to increase her knowledge of Latin and Greek. This she did and thus enrolled in the Collegiate Department in the Fall of 1861.

Coppin's decision to pursue the classical course, the only one that led to the B.A. degree, required talent, certainly, but also courage and a great deal of self-confidence and self-esteem. But perhaps, most of all, it required a nature that rebelled against the injustice of stereotypes without internalizing those stereotypes. By 1861, when Coppin embarked upon her undergraduate career, the classical tradition in America was firmly established. This tradition, with its canon of Homer, Plato, and Xenophon for ancient Greek, and Cicero, Caesar, and Vergil for ancient Latin, was pivotal in creating a racial, sexual, and class norm among the educated in America. Coppin, along with such future black alumnae of Oberlin as Anna Julia Cooper and Mary Church Terrell, was aware of the racial context of the classical tradition. Furthermore, Coppin was aware that mastery of classics was the barometer of intellectual capability. In more than one place in *Reminiscences* Coppin makes reference to John C. Calhoun, the proslavery vice president to John Quincy Adams and Andrew Jackson.[9] Coppin tells us that "it is said that John C. Calhoun made the remark that if there could be found a Negro that could conjugate a Greek verb, he would give up all his preconceived ideas of the inferiority of the Negro" (*Reminiscences*, 19). Anna Julia Cooper remarks that such racist assumptions drove African Americans to success: "Stung by such imputations as that of Calhoun that if a Negro could prove his ability to master the Greek subjunctive, he might vindicate his title to manhood, the newly liberated race first shot forward along this line with an energy and success which astonished its most sanguine friends" (Cooper, 260). Mary Church Terrell, a classmate of Cooper's, also had a brush with the stereotype of the intellectually inferior African:

> One day Matthew Arnold, the English writer, visited our class and Professor Frost asked me both to read the Greek and then to translate. After leaving the class Mr Arnold referred to the young lady who read the passage of Greek so well. Thinking it would interest the Englishman, Professor Frost told him I was of African descent. Thereupon Mr Arnold expressed the greatest surprise imaginable, because he said, he thought the tongue of the African was so thick he could not be taught to pronounce the Greek correctly.[10]

Coppin knew that her success at Oberlin in the classical course would disprove (although not dispel) this racial stereotype. She was cognizant of her position as a pioneer and its concomitant stress: "I never rose to recite in my classes at Oberlin but I felt that I had the honor of the whole African race upon my shoulders. I felt that, should I fail, it would be ascribed to the fact that I was colored." [11]

Racial stereotypes prevailed not only in classics, but also mathematics. Coppin speaks of her success in ancient Greek, but she was clearly most proud of her (and by extension, her race's) ability in mathematics. In a deliberate rebuttal to Calhoun's racist assumptions, Coppin describes her feelings before an examination in math: "I, indeed, was more anxious, for I had always heard that my race was good in the languages, but stumbled when they came to mathematics. Now I was always fond of a demonstration, and happened to get in the examination the very proposition I was well acquainted with; and so went that day out of the class with flying colors. . . . (*Reminiscences*, 15).

Perhaps the most telling testimony to the repression of knowledge caused by racism is Calhoun's ignorance of the academic successes of earlier generations of people of African descent. In the eighteenth century in Germany, Anton Amo held a doctorate from the University of Wittenberg; he was well-trained in languages, the classics, mathematics, and philosophy. Similarly, Francis Williams, a Jamaican, was educated by the Duke of Montagu at an English grammar school and continued with his education at Cambridge University. There he excelled in mathematics and classics. In the United States, Phillis Wheatley, largely self-taught in Latin, was proficient enough to recast Ovid's story of Niobe in Latin and then translate it. Coppin herself was aware that her "race was good in the languages," but she too knew little of African-American successes in mathematics.[12]

Coppin was also aware that very few black students enrolled at Oberlin. Because juniors and seniors in the Collegiate Department taught pupils in the Preparatory Department, she had the opportunity to observe that "with the exception of one here or there, all my pupils would be white."[13] Coppin frequently was the only student of color in her classes. Yet despite the stress familiar to many black students at predominantly white schools in any era, and the small black population, Coppin's memory of Oberlin was that of a biracial utopia. In *Reminiscences* she says that "I had been so long in Oberlin that I had forgotten about my color. . . .," and she

INTRODUCTION

relates the incident of a woman student from Maine who was so distressed by her sudden realization of the pain Coppin endured as a slave that she burst into tears. Coppin concludes, "Not another word was spoken by us. But those tears seemed to wipe out a little of what was wrong" (*Reminiscences*, 14).

On the whole, Coppin reconstructs her years at Oberlin in an optimistic framework, yet occasionally the racial politics of the time intrude upon her rosy recollections. As with the case of Mrs. Calvert and the music lessons, Coppin's peace was shattered by a summons, this time from the faculty. It was the custom for students in the Collegiate Department to gain teaching experience by teaching the preparatory classes. It was the faculty's intention to give her a class, but with reservations: "I was distinctly to understand that if the pupils rebelled against my teaching, they did not intend to force it." Coppin admits that "there was a little surprise on the faces of some when they came into class and saw the teacher," but due to her "training at the normal school" and her "own dear love of teaching," her class was a success (*Reminiscences*, 12). In fact, she was so successful that her class became increasingly popular and had to be divided into sections.

Still, the faculty was obviously aware of the strong Southern presence at their Ohio school and they were not willing to take the risk of losing the Southern enrollment by supporting a black woman teacher. There are other indications that Oberlin was not untouched by the racism current at the time. Emma Brown, a contemporary of Coppin's at Oberlin, remarked in a letter to a friend: "There is considerable prejudice here which I did not first perceive. . . ." (quoted in Sterling, 199). It is inconclusive from Coppin's account whether racial politics impinged upon residential life. Coppin lived in Ladies Hall during her first year; in her later years at Oberlin she lived first with the family of H. E. Peck and then with that of Charles Churchill. The reason she cites for her move was the deterioration of her health caused, she believed, by the lack of variety in the diet. Coppin's move probably did have more to do with health (and perhaps financial) considerations than racial politics. Hers is unlike the experience of black students who attended predominantly white colleges when Jim Crow laws and attitudes were in full force.

In pursuing a classical education, Coppin had to negotiate the equally tough obstacle of her gender. A sexist view of women's education was institutionalized at Oberlin. The classical course that led to the B.A. was a four-year curriculum firmly rooted in the philology of Latin and Greek and was known popularly as the "gentleman's course." For women, there was the literary course, or the "ladies course," a two-year curriculum leading to a certificate. Coppin says that the "faculty did not forbid a woman to take the gentleman's course, but they did not advise it" (*Reminiscences*, 12). When Anna Julia Cooper and Mary Church Terrell enrolled at Oberlin twenty years later, they found that the same attitude prevailed (Cooper, 49–50; Terrell, 32). In their study of the one hundred black students who attended Oberlin before the Civil War, Ellen Lawson and Marlene Merrill note that twelve out of the thirteen black women received the literary certificate.[14] Coppin's decision to enroll in the classical curriculum becomes all the more remarkable when we consider that no black woman had completed the classical course and graduated from Oberlin with a B.A. by 1861, the year Coppin enrolled in the Collegiate Department. Mary Jane Patterson was the first when she graduated in 1862. In terms of the self-construction of black womanhood, then, not much attention has been paid to the ramifications of the success of black women in the classical, that is, the gentleman's course. Mary Jane Patterson and Fanny Jackson Coppin did more than disprove race and gender stereotypes; they also bent the gender specificity of a classical education.

In the course of disproving racial stereotypes, Coppin fell in love with the content of classics. She accepted the challenge of the classical curriculum by first taking a "long breath" and holding a positive attitude: she was prepared for a "delightful contest" (*Reminiscences*, 12). Coppin shared this enthusiasm with the other black women who took the "gentleman's course" at Oberlin. Mary Church Terrell took more Greek than necessary because she "loved the Grecian authors"; a private letter from a fellow classmate reminds Terrell how fond she [Terrell] was of Vergil.[15] Anna Julia Cooper sprinkles references to classical authors and history throughout her work, *A Voice from the South*.

Even before Coppin graduated from Oberlin, she was recruited to teach at the Institute for Colored Youth. Coppin was well aware that the Institute was established by Quakers as a reactionary experiment to the prevailing racist assumptions of the day. The offer of the position was due both to Coppin's talent at Greek, Latin, and mathematics and to her proven success as a teacher. Coppin, even as an undergraduate at Oberlin, was a community education activist. In addition to her classes for preparatory students, she taught private music lessons, and during her last year at Oberlin she formed an evening class for the newly freed slaves, "where they might be taught to read and write" (*Reminiscences*, 18). The secret of Coppin's success as a teacher was the close identification she forged with her students as learners. Her delight did not come from her power as authority but from the success of her students. She was touched by the "painful" determination of the recently liberated slaves in her evening class and by their eagerness to learn (*Reminiscences*, 18). The word "delight" recurs throughout *Reminiscences*. Coppin describes her job at ICY as the "delightful task of teaching my people" (*Reminiscences*, 19–20). She "delighted" in her students' mastery of the canonical classical authors Caesar, Vergil, Cicero, Horace, and Xenophon. When she describes how titled Englishmen praised her students' proficiency in classics, her words nearly glow with pride. Certainly the efforts of the students bore some relation to their feeling for their teacher. From *Hints on Teaching*, in which Coppin argues against corporal punishment and the "empty-vessel" theory of pedagogy, it is clear that Coppin believes that there are no drives more powerful in the teaching process than respect, admiration, and love. Together they produce identification and transform the teacher-student polarity into a relation of reciprocity. Coppin communicated her feelings for her students through small, homely gestures. John Durham relates this story about his first meeting with Coppin: "Finally, she asked me what I intended to be after leaving school. I promptly answered; "A clerk!". . . She mildly protested, led me to a desk and sat in a chair next to mine. Nothing makes a child more at home with a teacher than this little act of kindly familiarity, and for the first time in my life I felt the influence of this great woman" (Durham).

At the same time that Coppin exulted in seeing her students master the intricacies of classical languages and mathematics, she also realized the value of choice in an education curriculum. She advocated, campaigned for, and established industrial and vocational curricula a full thirty years before Booker T. Washington did. However, she never wanted or intended for the classical curriculum to be supplanted by an industrial one. She firmly believed that it must be a matter of choice based on the talent, not the race, of the student.

Her industrial program was so successful that some people questioned the wisdom of the Quakers in establishing ICY as an academic (that is, a classical) institution in the first place. Coppin counters this line of reasoning by stressing the context of racial politics at the time ICY was established. She believes it was important and necessary to disprove prevailing racial stereotypes: "When they began this school, the whole south was a great industrial plant where the fathers taught the sons and the mothers taught the daughters but the mind was left in darkness. . . . So that the managers had builded [sic] wiser than many persons knew" (*Reminiscences*, 30). Coppin's love of the classics did not blind her to practical necessity. A recruitment team for black schools in Delaware, Maryland, and New Jersey arrived at ICY looking for teachers who were not required to know or teach classics, but who did need to know English. Coppin responded to their request: "Now it seemed best to give up the time spent in teaching Greek and devote it to the English studies" (*Reminiscences*, 22). Likewise she noted that there was a general trend for American public education to ignore industrial education. Coppin acknowledged that the deficiency existed for white students, but she asserted that it was far greater for black ones: "In Philadelphia, the only place at the time where a colored boy could learn a trade, was in the House of Refuge, or the Penitentiary" (*Reminiscences*, 23, 28). Student-centered in her standpoint as always, Coppin felt it was intellectual torture to force a carpenter to be a classics teacher: "It is cruel to make a teacher or preacher of a man who ought to be a printer or blacksmith, and that is exactly what we are obliged to do" (*Reminiscences*, 36).

Coppin strove constantly to keep education in touch with community needs. She realized early on that her success as a teacher was interrelated to her closeness to the black community. When she had her evening school for emancipated slaves at Oberlin, she regularly held fairs and exhibitions to publicize the accomplishments of her students, both black and white. The incorporation of an industrial curriculum at ICY came from community pressure after the success of Coppin's public fairs there. Her success was the product of both her organizational talents and community activism. Cornel West, in "The Dilemma of the Black Intellectual," discusses "the inability of black intellectuals to gain respect and support from the black community."[16] Coppin avoided this schism by never forgetting her own slave beginnings, by always maintaining a special affinity and respect for all people employed in domestic service, especially women, and by acknowledging the community and family members who had helped her. Coppin was most grateful to her aunt Sarah Orr, but she also remembers others, including Bishop Daniel Payne, who had given her money for tuition; Alfred Cope, who sent Coppin $80 when he heard of the teaching and work load she was carrying while a student at Oberlin; and Walter P. Hall, a member of Philadelphia's black community who donated $25 to Coppin's industrial school project. Although a brilliant teacher, speaker, administrator, and organizer, Coppin had no pretensions and never put on airs; she was always humble and respectful towards all, but especially towards those who gained knowledge through work and not institutional experience.

Coppin could not have known it then, but through her combination of community activism and intellectual pursuits she exemplified what now has been termed a core theme of black feminism. Patricia Hill Collins, in her summarization of the fundamental tenets of black feminism, observes that one of them is the "impossibility of separating intellectual inquiry from political activism."[17] In her vision of an educational scheme that included both the industrial and classical modes of knowledge, Coppin exhibited the both/and standpoint that is central to contemporary black feminism. In remarks made at a testimonial dinner on her behalf in

1902, Coppin said that she "had always had two schools—the Institute and the Philadelphia black community."[18]

In her academic and community activism, Coppin always put black women at the center. At her fairs and exhibitions, traditional skills—dressmaking, quilting, cooking—were always on prominent display. In describing her industrial department, Coppin states: "The following trades were being taught: for boys: bricklaying, plastering, carpentry, shoemaking, printing, tailoring. For girls: dressmaking, millinery, typewriting, stenography and classes in cooking, including boys and girls. Stenography and typewriting were also taught boys, as well as the girls" (*Reminiscences*, 25).

Although constrained by the gender-specific occupational market, Coppin still found a way to revolutionize industrial education. Furthermore, in her "Woman's Department" column for the *Christian Recorder*, Coppin urged women to look to nontraditional fields, to strive to be financially independent of men, and to consider opening their own businesses. Granted, in modern times the opportunities Coppin advocated for women—florist and millinery shops—are viewed as traditional women's work, but in 1878, the idea of black women being independent business owners must have been inspiring as well as revolutionary. Coppin also championed the newly established profession of nursing as one in which women could earn good wages.

Coppin demonstrated her own business acumen as well as her commitment to the black community when she undertook to save the *Christian Recorder*, the newspaper of the African Methodist Episcopal Church, from financial ruin. She planned a "World's Fair," and once again highlighted the artistic and creative talents of black women. The fair was a success and cleared the newspaper's debt. In addition to helping black women find occupations through her journalistic career tips, Coppin provided more concrete aid. In 1888, along with a committee of women from the Mother Bethel Church in Philadelphia, she opened a residence for homeless women. The women who resided there were also able to enroll in courses in nurses' training. Later, in 1894, Coppin opened the Women's Exchange and Girls' Home next door to her own house in Philadelphia. A residence for women as well as a business and school, it offered courses in cooking, dressmaking,

INTRODUCTION

and domestic economy, and items that had been made at the Home were sold at exhibitions.

Coppin always fought for the rights of all women, and of black women in particular. She often spoke at political rallies and advocated voting rights for women. She had experienced sexism from the time of her birth, but never allowed it to victimize her. Her experience at Oberlin demonstrated to her the sexism of the white academy. Moreover, sexism reared its ugly head at ICY. In 1869 Coppin was named the principal of the whole Institute upon the resignation of Ebenezer Bassett, who became the United States minister to Haiti. A senior male faculty member, Octavius V. Catto, objected to Coppin's appointment, but Alfred Cope, chair of the Board of Managers, supported it. He pointed out that, although Catto had more years at the school, Coppin was eminently more qualified for the position of principal. According to Levi Coppin's account, Catto objected to Coppin because of her gender and revealed his misogyny: "Octavious Cato [*sic*], a teacher in the scientific department informed the Managers of the Institute that he would not teach under a woman . . . " (Coppin, 352). Coppin herself never alluded to the bigoted behavior of her colleague, but characteristically presented an optimistic picture of complementary roles: "With Octavius V. Catto in charge of the boys department, and myself in charge of the girls—in connection with the principalship of the school—we had a strong working force" (*Reminiscences*, 22).

Whether a deliberate response or an unconscious reaction to the sexism she had experienced, Coppin eschewed the social company of men. By 1879, when she was in her late thirties, Coppin had a reputation for declining "the company of gentlemen, and was known to go and come anywhere, and everywhere alone" (Coppin, 354). Coppin herself never mentions any courtship, even that of her future husband. His account in *Unwritten History* is the only record we have, and it is tinged with male bravado as he congratulates himself on "winning" the unattainable Fanny Jackson. Levi Coppin had arranged with the janitor of the ICY that he would supplant the other man and escort Jackson home after the "World's Fair" in 1879. He continues: "I ventured the suggestion on a wager from my friend, that before the Fair closed,

I would have "John Williams"—the janitor—dismissed and take his place. I had a sort of fondness for daring, any way" (Coppin, 355). Most sources cite the date of their marriage as 21 December 1881.[19]

Once more rebelling against convention, Fanny Jackson Coppin was fifteen years older than her husband. Flouting conventions even further, she kept her position as principal at ICY and lived in Philadelphia while her husband held a pastorate at a church in Baltimore. Although Coppin wanted his wife to resign, she continued to work at ICY. He knew better than to insist, since her devotion to the school was abundantly clear.

Coppin publicly demonstrated her black feminist stance on two occasions. One was at the World's Congress of Representative Women, a predominantly white assembly that met in Chicago in 1893. In her address she foreshadows bell hooks and other contemporary black feminists who urge the inclusivity of black women's experience in women's history: "This conference cannot be indifferent to the history of colored women in America, . . . if we have been able to achieve anything by heroic living and thinking, all the more can you achieve it.[20] Later in the same address, Coppin speaks of the intellectual curiosity of black women:

> Our idea of getting an education did not come out of wanting to imitate anyone whatever. It grew out of the uneasiness and restlessness of the desires we felt within us; the desire to know, not just a little, but a great deal. We wanted to know how to calculate an eclipse, to know what Hesiod and Livy thought; we wished to know the best thoughts of the best minds that lived with us; not merely to gain an honest livelihood, but from a God-given love of all that is beautiful and best, and because we thought we could do it. (Sewall, 716)

The other occasion for Coppin's acknowledgment of her black feminism was her speech before the Working Women's Guild of the New Century Club in Philadelphia. John Durham reports Coppin's words: "During my entire life, I have suffered from two disadvantages: first that I am a woman; second that I am a Negro." Durham continues with his summary of Coppin's address:

"She told them that she had no favors to ask for herself; that whether white people willed it or not, she could not be prevented from striving to measure up to her own standard of usefulness and of mental and moral growth. She was there to speak in behalf of her sisters and their sisters who were not so endowed. . . ." (Durham).

The altruism that was the core of Coppin's black feminism was also the focus of her educational philosophy. Driven by the best interests of her students, Coppin centered her administrative style and pedagogical philosophy on their needs. When the Board of Managers of ICY instituted tuition fees in 1866, Coppin immediately foresaw the potential for financial hardship for some families and the potential for exclusion of the very pupils who would most benefit from ICY's academic programs. Coppin refused to dismiss students who were delinquent in their tuition payments. Using an administrative loophole in the design of the tuition plan, Coppin put enough pressure on the Board of Managers to force them to abolish the practice of charging tuition fees.

In a similar vein, Coppin was adamantly opposed to corporal punishment, and as principal did away with it at ICY. Here again she ran into opposition from her colleague Catto, who was against the new rule. Coppin believed in reciprocal respect, and maintained that students who were shown respect would return respect to their teachers. She stated, "A child knows well when a teacher is kind and considerate of him" (*Reminiscences*, 56). In keeping with this philosophy of respect, Coppin firmly states in *Hints on Teaching*: "Never let the word 'dumb' be used in your class, or anything said disrespectful of parents or guardians who may have helped the child" (*Reminiscences*, 41). Such respect and kindness would come in handy when a teacher met a recalcitrant student: "Whenever a pupil has spoken disrespectfully to a teacher and the teacher can say with truth, 'do I not always speak kindly and politely to you?' The case is won without any more comment" (*Reminiscences*, 49).

Yet Coppin was not "soft"; she was remembered by former students as a strict disciplinarian. She expelled a student in April 1879 for "impertinent behavior," and she never hesitated to dismiss any student who was disrespectful or possessed of "improper charac-ter."[21] It was her firm belief that the character of the students reflected the character of the school.

In addition to being student-centered, Coppin's educational philosophy was decidedly proactive. Coppin did not accept the "empty-vessel" theory of education, but rather saw the student as an active participant in the learning process. In *Hints on Teaching*, Coppin remarks: "Again we want to lift education out of the slough of the passive voice. Little Mary goes to school to be educated. . . . It is too often the case that the passive voice has the right of way, whereas in the very beginning we should call into active service all faculties of mind and body" (*Reminiscences*, 39).

Again under "Methods of Instruction" in *Hints On Teaching*, Coppin makes clear her preference for the proactive: "I am always sorry to hear that such and such a person is going to school to be educated" (Reminiscences, 44).

In many places throughout *Hints On Teaching*, Coppin fore-shadows the pedagogical principles that form the foundations of progressive educational theories: literacy, whole language (a holis-tic approach to teaching and learning literacy that uses psycholin-guistic theory to encourage the natural learning of reading and writing), and cooperative learning. Coppin welded her own strug-gle for an education to an unshakable belief in her people. For Coppin, education was the heart of character transformation and the fulcrum of social reform. Coppin believed in the intuitive moral goodness and intellectual curiosity of black people, and always emphasized that of black women. Her final words at the World's Congress of Representative Women encapsulates her black feminist thought and her educational philosophy:

There was a single word used in the address that I heard this evening that I can not hear without having permission to reply. What is that word? We, as you know, are classed among working people, and so when the days of slavery were over, and we wanted an education, people said, "What are you going to do with an edu-cation?" You know yourselves you have been met with a great many arguments of that kind. Why educate the woman—what will

she do with it? An impertinent question, and an unwise one.
Rather ask, "What will she be with it?" (Sewall, 716)

Fanny Jackson Coppin testified throughout her life to the intellectual curiosity, moral strength, and community devotion of all
black women.

NOTES

[1]Fannie Barrier Williams, "Club Movement among Negro Women," in
Progress of a Race, ed. J. W. Gibson and W. H. Crogman (1902; reprint,
Miami, Fla.: Mnemosyne Publishing, 1969), 201.

[2]Fanny Jackson Coppin, *Reminiscences of School Life, and Hints on
Teaching* (Philadelphia: AME Book Concern, 1913), 9–10; hereafter cited
in text as *Reminiscences*.

[3]Levi J. Coppin, *Unwritten History* (1919; reprint, New York: Negro
Universities Press, a division of Greenwood Press, 1968), 362–63; hereafter cited in text as Coppin. The *Philadelphia Tribune* (5 March 1993)
attributes this statement to Fanny Jackson Coppin, but I was only able to
find it in Levi Coppin's autobiography. Since he borrowed other oral
statements and expressions (such as the title of his autobiography) from
Fanny, it is possible he remembered it from one of Fanny's lectures. In
any case, he does not give her credit for it.

[4]John Durham, "Mrs. Coppin and Her Work," *New York Age* (8
November 1890), no page number; hereafter cited in text as Durham.

[5]The evidence for Coppin's family background is assembled in Linda
Perkins, *Fanny Jackson Coppin and the Institute For Colored Youth,
1865–1902* (New York: Garland Press, 1987), 14–15, 50n1–4; hereafter
cited in text.

[6]According to an erroneous recollection of A. V. Churchill (with
whose family Coppin lived while a student at Oberlin), Coppin bought
her own and her mother's freedom for $1000. See Perkins, 50n3.

[7]A. V. Churchill, "Midwestern: The Colored People," *Northwest Ohio
Quarterly* 25 (1953): 166. Perkins recommends caution when reading or
using Churchill's recollections. He claims that Coppin lived with the
Churchill family and took care of him for a long time. But as Perkins
points out, Coppin was a student at Oberlin at the time and only lived
with the Churchill family for six months (Perkins, 50n3).

[8]John W. Cromwell, *The Negro in American History* (Washington,
D.C.: American Negro Academy, 1914), 213.

[9]*Reminiscences*, 19, 30. Anna Julia Cooper also is anxious to point out the absurdity of Calhoun's statement. See Cooper, *A Voice from the South* (1892; reprint, New York: Oxford University Press, 1988), 260–61; hereafter cited in text.

[10]Mary Church Terrell, *A Colored Woman in a White World* (Washington, D.C.: Ransdell Publishers, 1940), 41; hereafter cited as Terrell.

[11]*Reminiscences*, 15. Mary Church Terrell, who attended Oberlin College from 1881 to 1884, had similar feelings, although at a younger age: "At that time I was the only colored girl in the class, and I felt I must hold high the banner of my race" (Terrell, 21).

[12]*Reminiscences*, 15. According to Perkins, 56, Coppin was competent in Greek, Latin, Sanskrit, and French.

[13]*Reminiscences*, 18–19. According to R. Fletcher, *A History of Oberlin College*, vol. 2 (Oberlin, Ohio: Oberlin College, 1943), 536, "In the spring of 1859 only thirty-two Negroes were reported at a time when the student body numbered 1200 altogether." Emma Brown, who was at Oberlin at the same time as Coppin, Mary Jane Patterson (whose 1862 graduation from Oberlin is on record as the first B.A. granted to a black woman by a U.S. college), and Edmonia Lewis (another black attendee of Oberlin who later became a sculptor and founder of a sculpting studio in Rome), remarked, "There are very few colored students—that is comparatively speaking. . . . I believe there are about twelve other colored students in the college and I suppose twenty in the preparatory. I wish there were more" (Dorothy Sterling, *We Are Your Sisters* [New York: Norton, 1984], 200; hereafter cited in text).

[14]Ellen Lawson and Marlene Merrill, "The Antebellum 'Talented Thousandth': Black College Students at Oberlin before the Civil War," *Journal of Negro Education* 52, no. 2 (1983): 151–52.

[15]Terrell, 40–41. Letter from Harriet C. Andrews to Terrell, dated 24 October 1930 and preserved with Terrell's papers in the Library of Congress.

[16]Cornel West, "The Dilemma of the Black Intellectual," *Cultural Critique* 1 (1985): 112.

[17]Patricia Hill Collins, "Feminism in the Twentieth Century," in *Black Women in America*, vol. 1, ed. Darlene Clark Hine (Brooklyn, N.Y.: Carlson Publishing, 1993), 419.

[18]Linda M. Perkins, "Quaker Beneficence and Black Control: The Institute for Colored Youth, 1852–1903," in *New Perspectives on Black Educational History*, ed. Vincent P. Franklin and James D. Anderson (Boston: G.K. Hall, 1978), 40.

[19]Levi Coppin's account says he and his wife were married in 1887, but this is most likely a typographical error. An 1882 issue of *Christian Reader* refers to Fannie J. Coppin as "Mrs. Fannie Coppin, nee Jackson."

[20]Coppin's address appears in May Wright Sewall, *World's Congress of Representative Women*, vol. 2 (Chicago: n.p., 1893), 715; hereafter cited as Sewall.

[21]Institute for Colored Youth's Board of Managers' Meeting Minutes, April 1879, in the Friends Historical Library at Swarthmore College.

Mrs. FANNY JACKSON COPPIN

REMINISCENCES

_of_

School Life, and Hints
on Teaching

_By_ **_Fanny Jackson-Coppin_**
Philadelphia, Pa., U.S.A.

Philadelphia, Pa.
A. M. E. Book Concern
631 Pine St.

INSCRIPTION

THIS BOOK IS INSCRIBED TO MY BELOVED AUNT

SARAH ORR CLARK

WHO, WORKING AT SIX DOLLARS A MONTH
SAVED ONE HUNDRED AND TWENTY-FIVE
DOLLARS, AND BOUGHT MY FREEDOM

CONTENTS

PART I.

INTRODUCTION.

CONTENTS

———

PART II.

PREFACE.

HE author of this work was frequently urged by friends to write, for publication, something that would present a view of the writer's early life, as well as give some of her methods of imparting the intellectual and moral instruction that has proved so eminently successful in influencing and moulding so many lives.

After much persuasion, the work was begun, and carried forward to its present stage.

The final work of editing and directing its publication has fallen into other hands, and however inefficiently done, is a loving service, willingly performed, and sent forth with a hope that it may accomplish much good, especially in the way of inspiring those readers who are anxious to make the most of their opportunities.

L. J. COPPIN.

PART I

I.

AUTOBIOGRAPHY: A SKETCH.

THERE are some few points in my life which, "some forlorn and ship-wrecked brother seeing, may take heart again."

We used to call our grand-mother "mammy," and one of my earliest recollections—I must have been about three years old—is, I was sent to keep my mammy company. It was in a little one-room cabin. We used to go up a ladder to the loft where we slept.

Mammy used to make a long prayer every night before going to bed; but not one word of all she said do I remember except the one word "offspring." She would ask God to bless her offspring. This word remained with me, for, I wondered what offspring meant.

Mammy had six children, three boys and three girls. One of these, Lucy, was my mother. Another one of them, Sarah, was purchased by my grandfather, who first saved money and bought himself, then four of his children. Sarah went to work at six dollars a

9

month, saved one hundred and twenty-five dollars, and bought little Frances, having taken a great liking to her, for on account of my birth, my grandfather refused to buy my mother; and so I was left a slave in the District of Columbia, where I was born.

In my childhood, I had two severe burnings. I understand that at my christening the old folks gave a large party, and I was tied in a chair and placed near the stove. At night, when they took off my stocking, the whole skin from the side of the leg next the stove peeled off.

At another time, when mother was out at work for the day, mammy had charge of the baby. When mother returned, mammy exclaimed: "Here, Lucy, take your child, it's the crossest baby I ever saw." When I was undressed at night, it was found that a coal of fire from mammy's pipe had fallen into the baby's bosom, and had burned itself deep into the flesh. There were no Day Nurseries then.

Passing over years, I distinctly remember having chills and fever. Sometimes I would be taken with a shaking ague on the street, and would have to sit down upon a doorstep until I would stop shaking enough to go on my way. Then, I would have to go to bed, as I could not endure the fever and headache that would follow. When my aunt had finally saved up the hundred and twenty-five dollars, she bought me and sent me to New Bedford, Mass., where another aunt lived, who promised to get me a place to work for my board, and get a little education if I could. She put me out to work, at a place where I was allowed to go to school when I was not at work. But I could not go on wash day, nor ironing day, nor cleaning day, and this interfered with my progress. There were no Hamptons, and no night schools then.

Finally, I found a chance to go to Newport with Mrs. Elizabeth Orr, an aunt by marriage, who offered me a home with her and a better chance at school. I went with her, but I was not satisfied to be a burden on her small resources. I was now fourteen years old, and felt that I ought to take care of myself. So I found a permanent place in the family of Mr. George H. Calvert, a great grandson of Lord Baltimore, who settled Maryland. His wife was Elizabeth Stuart, a descendant of Mary, Queen of Scots. Here I had one hour every other afternoon in the week to take some private lessons, which I did of Mrs. Little. After that, I attended for a few months the public colored school which was taught by Mrs. Gavitt. I thus prepared myself to enter the examination for the Rhode Island State Normal School, under Dana P. Colburn; the school was then located at Bristol, R. I. Here, my eyes were first opened on the subject of teaching. I said to myself, is it possible that teaching can be made so interesting as this! But, having finished the course of study there, I felt that I had just begun to learn; and, hearing of Oberlin College, I made up my mind to try and get there. I had learned a little music while at Newport, and had mastered the elementary studies of the piano and guitar. My aunt in Washington still helped me, and I was able to pay my way to Oberlin, the course of study there being the same as that at Harvard College. Oberlin was then the only College in the United States where colored students were permitted to study.

The faculty did not forbid a woman to take the gentleman's course, but they did not advise it. There was plenty of Latin and Greek in it, and as much mathematics as one could shoulder. Now, I took a long breath and prepared for a delightful contest. All went smoothly until I was in the junior year in College. Then, one day, the Faculty sent for me— ominous request—and I was not slow in obeying it. It was a custom in Oberlin that forty students from the junior and senior classes were employed to teach the preparatory classes. As it was now time for the juniors to begin their work, the Faculty informed me that it was their purpose to give me a class, but I was to distinctly understand that if the pupils rebelled against my teaching, they did not intend to force it. Fortunately for my training at the normal school, and my own dear love of teaching, tho there was a little surprise on the faces of some when they came into the class, and saw the teacher, there were no signs of rebellion. The class went on increasing in numbers until it had to be divided, and I was given both divisions. One of the divisions ran up again, but the Faculty decided that I had as much as I could do, and it would not allow me to take any more work.

When I was within a year of graduation, an application came from a Friends' school in Philadelphia for a colored woman who could teach Greek, Latin, and higher mathematics. The answer returned was: "We have the woman, but you must wait a year for her."

Then began a correspondence with Alfred Cope, a saintly character, who, having found out what my work in college was, teaching my classes in college, besides sixteen private music scholars, and keeping up my work in the senior class, immediately sent me a check for eighty dollars, which wonderfully lightened my burden as a poor student.

I shall never forget my obligation to Bishop Daniel A. Payne, of the African Methodist Episcopal Church, who gave me a scholarship of nine dollars a year upon entering Oberlin.

My obligation to the dear people of Oberlin can never be measured in words. When President Finney met a new student, his first words were: "Are you a Christian? and if not, why not?" He would follow you up with an intelligent persistence that could not be resisted, until the question was settled.

When I first went to Oberlin I boarded in what was known as the Ladies' Hall, and altho the food was good, yet, I think, that for lack of variety I began to run down in health. About this time I was invited to spend a few weeks in the family of Professor H. E. Peck, which ended in my staying a few years, until the independence of the Republic of Hayti was recognized, under President Lincoln, and Professor Peck was sent as the first U. S. Minister to that interesting country; then the family was broken up, and I was invited by Professor and Mrs. Charles H. Churchill to spend the remainder of my time, about six months, in their family. The influence upon my life in these two Christian homes, where I was regarded as an honored member of the family circle, was a potent factor in forming the character which was to stand the test of the new and strange conditions of my life in Philadelphia. I had been so long in Oberlin that I had forgotten about my color, but I was sharply reminded of it when, in a storm of rain, a Philadelphia street car conductor forbid my entering a car that did not have on it "for colored people," so I had to wait in the storm until one came in which colored people could ride. This was my first unpleasant experience in Philadelphia. Visiting Oberlin not long after my work began in Philadelphia, President Finney asked me how I was growing in grace; I told him that I was growing as fast as the American people would let me. When told of some of the conditions which were meeting me, he seemed to think it unspeakable.

At one time, at Mrs. Peck's, when we girls were sitting on the floor getting out our Greek, Miss Sutherland, from Maine, suddenly stopped, and, looking at me, said: "Fanny Jackson, were you ever a slave?" I said yes; and she burst into tears. Not another word was spoken by us. But those tears seemed to wipe out a little of what was wrong.

I never rose to recite in my classes at Oberlin but I felt that I had the honor of the whole African race upon my shoulders. I felt that, should I fail, it would be ascribed to the fact that I was colored. At one time, when I had quite a signal triumph in Greek, the Professor of Greek concluded to visit the class in mathematics and see how we were getting along. I was particularly anxious to show him that I was as safe in mathematics as in Greek.

I, indeed, was more anxious, for I had always heard that my race was good in the languages, but stumbled when they came to mathematics. Now, I was always fond of a demonstration, and happened to get in the examination the very proposition that I was well acquainted with; and so went that day out of the class with flying colors.

I was elected class poet for the Class Day exercises, and have the kindest remembrance of the dear ones who were my classmates. I never can forget the courtesies of the three Wright brothers; of Professor Pond, of Dr. Lucien C. Warner, of Doctor Kincaid, the Chamberland girls, and others, who seemed determined that I should carry away from Oberlin nothing but most pleasant memories of my life there.

Recurring to my tendency to have shaking agues every fall and spring in Washington, I often used to tell my aunt that if she bought me according to my weight, she certainly had made a very poor bargain. For I was not only as slim as a match, but, as the Irishman said, I was as slim as two matches.

While I was living with Mrs. Calvert at Newport, R. I., I went with her regularly to bathe in the ocean, and after this I never had any more shakes or chills. It was contrary to law for colored persons to bathe at the regular bathing hour, which was the only safe hour to go into the ocean, but, being in the employ of Mrs. Calvert, and going as her servant, I was not prohibited from taking the baths which proved so beneficial to me. She went and returned in her carriage.

After this I began to grow stronger, and take on flesh. Mrs. Calvert sometimes took me out to drive with her; this also helped me to get stronger.

Being very fond of music, my aunt gave me permission to hire a piano and have it at her house, and I used to go there and take lessons. But, in the course of time, it became noticeable to Mrs. Calvert that I was absent on Wednesdays at a certain hour, and that without permission. So, on one occasion, when I was absent, Mrs. Calvert inquired of the cook as to my whereabouts, and directed her to send me to her upon my return that I might give an explanation. When the cook informed me of what had transpired, I was very much afraid that something quite unpleasant awaited me. Upon being questioned, I told her the whole truth about the matter. I told Mrs. Calvert that I had been taking lessons for some time, and that I had already advanced far enough to play the little organ in the Union Church. Instead of being terribly scolded, as I had feared, Mrs. Calvert said: "Well, Fanny, when people will go ahead, they cannot be kept back; but, if you had asked me, you might have had the piano here." Mrs. Calvert taught me to sew beautifully and to darn, and to take care of laces. My life there was most happy, and I never would have left her, but it was in me to get an education and to teach my people. This idea was deep in my soul. Where it came from I cannot tell, for I had never had any exhortations, nor any lectures which influenced me to take this course. It must have been born in me. At Mrs. Calvert's, I was in contact with people of refinement and education. Mr. Calvert was a perfect gentleman, and a writer of no mean ability. They had no children, and this gave me an opportunity to come very near to Mrs. Calvert, doing for her many things which otherwise a daughter would have done. I loved her and she loved me. When I was about to leave her to go to the Normal School, she said to me: "Fanny, will money keep you?" But that deep-seated purpose to get an education and become a teacher to my people, yielded to no inducement of comfort or temporary gain. During the time that I attended the Normal School in Rhode Island, I got a chance to take some private lessons in French, and eagerly availed myself of the opportunity. French was not in the Oberlin curriculum, but there was a professor there who taught it privately, and I continued my studies under him, and so was able to complete the course and graduate with a French essay. Freedmen now began to pour into Ohio from the South, and some of them settled in the township of Oberlin. During my last year at the college, I formed an evening class for them, where they might be taught to read and write. It was deeply touching to me to see old men painfully following the simple words of spelling; so intensely eager to learn. I felt that for such people to have been kept in the darkness of ignorance was an unpardonable sin, and I rejoiced that even then I could enter measurably upon the course in life which I had long ago chosen. Mr. John M. Langston, who afterwards became Minister to Hayti, was then practicing law at Oberlin. His comfortable home was always open with a warm welcome to colored students, or to any who cared to share his hospitality.

I went to Oberlin in 1860, and was graduated in August, 1865, after having spent five and a half years.

The years 1860 and 1865 were years of unusual historic importance and activity. In '60 the immortal Lincoln was elected, and in '65 the terrible war came to a close, but not until freedom for all the slaves in America had been proclaimed, and that proclamation made valid by the victorious arms of the Union party. In the year 1863 a very bitter feeling was exhibited against the colored people of the country, because they were held responsible for the fratricidal war then going on. The riots in New York especially gave evidence of this ill feeling. It was in this year that the faculty put me to teaching.

Of the thousands then coming to Oberlin for an education, a very few were colored. I knew that, with the exception of one here or there, all my pupils would be white; and so they were. It took a little moral courage on the part of the faculty to put me in my place against the old custom of giving classes only to white students. But, as I have said elsewhere, the matter was soon settled and became an overwhelming success. How well do I remember the delighted look on the face of Principal Fairchild when he came into the room to divide my class, which then numbered over eighty. How easily a colored teacher might be put into some of the public schools. It would only take a little bravery, and might cause a little surprise, but wouldn't be even a nine days' wonder.

And now came the time for me to leave Oberlin, and start in upon my work at Philadelphia.

In the year 1837, the Friends of Philadelphia had established a school for the education of colored youth in higher learning. To make a test whether or not the Negro was capable of acquiring any considerable degree of education. For it was one of the strongest arguments in the defense of slavery, that the Negro was an inferior creation; formed by the Almighty for just the work he was doing. It is said that John C. Calhoun made the remark, that if there could be found a Negro that could conjugate a Greek verb, he would give up all his preconceived ideas of the inferiority of the Negro. Well, let's try him, and see, said the fair-minded Quaker people. And for years this institution, known as the Institute for Colored Youth, was visited by interested persons from different parts of the United States and Europe. Here I was given the delightful task of teaching my own people, and how delighted I was to see them mastering Caesar, Virgil, Cicero, Horace and Xenophon's Anabasis. We also taught New Testament Greek. It was customary to have public examinations once a year, and when the teachers were thru examining their classes, any interested person in the audience was requested to take it up, and ask questions. At one of such examinations, when I asked a titled Englishman to take the class and examine it, he said: "They are more capable of examining me, their proficiency is simply wonderful."

One visiting friend was so pleased with the work of the students in the difficult metres in Horace that he afterwards sent me, as a present, the Horace which he used in college. A learned Friend from Germantown, coming into a class in Greek, the first aorist, passive and middle, being so neatly and correctly written at one board, while I, at the same time, was hearing a class recite, exclaimed: "Fanny, I find thee driving a coach and six." As it is much more difficult to drive a coach and six, than a coach and one, I took it as a compliment. But I was especially glad to know that the students were doing their work so well as to justify Quakers in their fair-minded opinion of them. General O. C. Howard, who was brought in at one time by one of the managers to hear an examination in Virgil, remarked that Negroes in trigonometry and the classics might well share in the triumphs of their brothers on the battlefield.

When I came to the School, the Principal of the

Institute was Ebenezer D. Bassett, who for fourteen years had charge of the work. He was a graduate of the State Normal School of Connecticut, and was a man of unusual natural and acquired ability, and an accurate and ripe scholar; and, withal, a man of great modesty of character. Many are the reminiscences he used to give of the visits of interested persons to the school: among these was a man who had written a book to prove that the Negro was not a man. And, having heard of the wonderful achievements of this Negro school, he determined to come and see for himself what was being accomplished. He brought a friend with him, better versed in algebra than himself, and asked Mr. Bassett to bring out his highest class. There was in the class at that time Jesse Glasgow, a very black boy. All he asked was a chance. Just as fast as they gave the problems, Jesse put them on the board with the greatest ease. This decided the fate of the book, then in manuscript form, which, so far as we know, was never published. Jesse Glasgow afterwards found his way to the University of Edinburgh, Scotland.

In the year 1869, Mr. Bassett was appointed United States Minister to Hayti by President Grant; leaving the principalship of the Institute vacant. Now, Octavius V. Catto, a professor in the school, and myself, had an opportunity to keep the school up to the same degree of proficiency that it attained under its former Principal and to carry it forward as much as possible.

About this time we were visited by a delegation of school commissioners, seeking teachers for schools in Delaware, Maryland and New Jersey. These teachers were not required to know and teach the classics, but they were expected to come into an examination upon the English branches, and to have at their tongue's end the solution of any abstruse problem in the three R's which their examiners might be inclined to ask them. And now, it seemed best to give up the time spent in teaching Greek and devote it to the English studies.

As our young people were now about to find a ready field in teaching, it was thought well to introduce some text books on school management, and methods of teaching, and thoroughly prepare our students for normal work. At this time our faculty was increased by the addition of Richard T. Greener, a graduate of Harvard College, who took charge of the English Department, and Edward Bouchet, a graduate of Yale College, and also of the Sheffield Scientific School, who took charge of the scientific department. Both of these young men were admirably fitted for their work. And, with Octavius V. Catto in charge of the boys' department, and myself in charge of the girls —in connection with the principalship of the school— we had a strong working force.

I now instituted a course in normal training, which at first consisted only of a review of English studies, with the theory of teaching, school management and methods. But the inadequacy of this course was so apparent that when it became necessary to reorganize the Preparatory Departments, it was decided to put this work into the hands of the normal students, who would thus have ample practice in teaching and governing under daily direction and correction. These students became so efficient in their work that they were sought for and engaged to teach long before they finished their course of study.

Richard Humphreys, the Friend—Quaker—who gave the first endowment with which to found the school, stipulated that it should not only teach higher literary studies, but that a Mechanical and Industrial Department, including Agriculture, should come within the scope of its work. The wisdom of this thoughtful and far-seeing founder has since been amply demonstrated. At the Centennial Exhibition in 1876, the foreign exhibits of work done in trade schools opened the eyes of the directors of public education in America as to the great lack existing in our own system of education. If this deficiency was apparent as it related to the white youth of the country, it was far more so as it related to the colored.

In Philadelphia, the only place at the time where a colored boy could learn a trade, was in the House of Refuge, or the Penitentiary!

And now began an eager and intensely earnest crusade to supply this deficiency in the work of the Institute for Colored Youth.

The teachers of the Institute now vigorously applied their energies in collecting funds for the establishment of an Industrial Department, and in this work they had the encouragement of the managers of the school, who were as anxious as we that the greatly needed department should be established.

In instituting this department, a temporary organization was formed, with Mr. Theodore Starr as President, Miss Anna Hallowell as Treasurer, and myself as Field Agent.

The Academic Department of the Institute had been so splendidly successful in proving that the Negro youth was equally capable as others in mastering a higher education, that no argument was necessary to establish its need, but the broad ground of education by which the masses must become self-supporting was, to me, a matter of painful anxiety. Frederick Douglass once said, it was easier to get a colored boy into a lawyer's office than into a blacksmith shop; and on account of the inflexibility of the Trades Unions, this condition of affairs still continues, making it necessary for us to have our own "blacksmith shop."

The minds of our people had to be enlightened upon the necessity of industrial education.

Before all the literary societies and churches where they would hear me; in Philadelphia and the suburban towns; in New York, Washington and everywhere, when invited to speak, I made that one subject my theme. To equip an industrial plant is an expensive thing, and knowing that much money would be needed, I made it a rule to take up a collection wheresoever I spoke. But I did not urge anyone to give more than a dollar, for the reason I wanted the masses to have an opportunity to contribute their small offerings, before going to those who were able to give larger sums. Never shall I forget the encouragement given me when a colored man, whom I did not know, met me and said: "I have heard of your Industrial School project, come to me for twenty-five dollars. That man was Walter P. Hall; all honor to him.

In preparing for the industrial needs of the boys, the girls were not neglected. It was not difficult to find competent teachers of sewing and cooking for the girls.

Dressmaking on the Taylor system was introduced with great success, and cooking was taught by the most improved methods.

As the work advanced, other trades were added, and those already undertaken were expanded and perfected.

When the Industrial Department was fully established, the following trades were being taught: For boys: bricklaying, plastering, carpentry, shoemaking, printing and tailoring. For the girls: dressmaking, millinery, typewriting, stenography and classes in cooking, including both boys and girls. Stenography and typewriting were also taught the boys, as well as the girls.

Having taught certain trades, it was now necessary to find work for those who had learned them, which proved to be no easy task.

It was decided to put on exhibition, in one of the

rooms of the dormitory, specimens of the work of our girls in any trade in which they had become proficient, and we thus started an Industrial Exchange for their work. Those specimens consisted of work from the sewing, millinery and cooking departments.

In order to get the work of the Exchange more prominently before our people, I asked and obtained permission to hold some public exhibitions of it in the lecture rooms of the churches.

Those who sent their work to the Exchange were asked to send articles that would be salable.

Our white friends were invited to come and inspect the work of the Exchange. Some of the exhibits were found to be highly creditable, and many encouraging words were given to those who prepared them. There is one class of women, for whom no trades are provided, but who are expected to do their work without any special preparation; and these are the women in domestic service. I have always felt a deep sympathy with such persons, for I believe that they are capable of making a most honorable record. I therefore conceived a plan of holding some receptions for them, where the honorableness of their work and the necessity of doing it well might be discussed. I earnestly hoped that no one should be ashamed of the word servant, but should learn what great opportunity for doing good there is for those who serve others.

There is, and always must be, a large number of people who must depend upon this class of employment for a living, and there is every reason, therefore, why they should be especially prepared for it. A woman should not only know how to cook in an ordinary way, but she should have some idea of the chemical properties of the food she cooks. The health of those whom she serves depends much upon the nutritive qualities of the food which she prepares. It is possible to burn all the best out of a beefsteak, and leave a pork chop with those elements which should have been neutralized by thorough cooking.

A housemaid should know enough about sanitation to appreciate the difference between well ventilated sleeping rooms and those where impure air prevails.

I have often thought, as I sat in churches, that janitors should be better prepared for their work by being taught the difference between pure air and air with a strong infusion of coal gas.

Then, besides the mere knowledge of how to do things, morality and Christian courtesy are valuable assets for those who serve others. Thoughtful kindness for those we serve is always in place.

As a means of preparation for this work, which I may call an Industrial Crusade, I studied Political Economy for two years under Dr. William Elder, who was a disciple of Mr. Henry C. Carey, the eminent writer on the doctrine of Protective Tariff.

In the year 1879 the Board of Education of Philadelphia, instructed and admonished by the exhibit of work done in the schools of Europe, as exhibited in the Centennial exhibition of '76, began to consider what they were doing to train their young people in the industrial arts and trades. The comparison was not very gratifying. The old apprenticeship system had silently glided away, and merchants declared that under the pressure of competition they were not able to compete with other merchants, nor were they able to stand the waste made by those who did not know how to handle the new material economically. At a meeting of some of the public school directors and heads of some of the educational institutions, I was asked to tell what was being done in Philadelphia for the industrial education of the colored youth. It may well be understood I had a tale to tell. And I told them the only places in the city where a colored boy could learn a trade was in the House of Refuge or the Penitentiary, and the sooner he became incorrigible and got into the Refuge, or committed a crime and got into the Penitentiary, the more promising it would be for his industrial training. It was to me a serious occasion. I so expressed myself. As I saw building after building going up in this city, and not a single colored hand employed in the constructions, it made the occasion a very serious one to me. Nor could I be comforted by what the Irishman said, that all he had to do was to put some bricks into a hod and carry them up on the building, and there sat a gentleman who did all the work. The arguments which I then gave were chiefly those which I afterwards repeated in my appeal to the citizens of Philadelphia, and which I elsewhere reproduce.

The next day Mrs. Elizabeth Whitney, the wife of one of the school directors, drove up to my school and said: Mrs. Coppin, I was there last night and heard what you had to say about the limitations of the colored youth, and I am here to say, if the colored people will go ahead and start a school for the purpose of having the colored youth taught this greatly needed education, you will find plenty of friends to help you. Here are fifty dollars to get you started, and you will find as much behind it as you need.

We only needed a feather's weight of encouragement to take up the burden. We started out at once. A temporary organization was formed, with Anna Hallowell as treasurer and Mr. Theodore Starr as president. I was unwilling to be the custodian of any large amount of money which might be begged from the poor colored people, and so myself and those who helped me asked each one to give only one dollar. I cannot mention the incidents which arose during this struggle and endeavor to supply this greatly needed want. We carried on an industrial crusade which never ended until we saw a building devoted to the purpose of teaching trades. For the managers of the Institute, seeing the need of the work, threw themselves into this new business, after their thirty previous years working for the colored youth. Our money in the end amounted to nearly three thousand dollars, and of this we have always been justly very glad. We could have had twenty times as much more, except for my backwardness and unwillingness to press poor people beyond what I thought they could give. Three thousand dollars was a mere drop in the bucket, but it was a great deal to us, who had seen it collected in small sums—quarters, dollars, etc. It was a delightful scene to us to pass thru that school where ten trades were being taught, altho in primitive fashion, the limited means of the Institute precluding the use of machinery. The managers always refused to take any money from the State, altho it was frequently offered.

Many were the ejaculations of satisfaction at this busy hive of industry. "Ah," said some, "this is the way the school should have begun, the good Quaker people began at the wrong end." Not so, for when they began this school, the whole South was a great industrial plant where the fathers taught the sons and the mothers taught the daughters, but the mind was left in darkness. That is the reason that John C. Calhoun is said to have remarked: "If you will show me a Negro who can conjugate a Greek verb, I will give up all my preconceived ideas of him." So that the managers had builded wiser than many persons knew.

In the fall of the same year, namely, in November, '79, as a means of bringing the idea of industrial education and self help practically before the colored people of the United States, I undertook the work of helping an enterprise, namely, *The Christian Recorder*, edited and published by colored men at 631 Pine street, Philadelphia. I here reproduce the plea made thirty-four years ago:

The Publication Department of *The Christian Re-*

corder is weighed down by a comparatively small debt,
which cripples its usefulness and thus threatens its existence. This paper finds its way into many a dark
hamlet in the South, where no one ever heard of the
Philadelphia *Bulletin* or the *New York Tribune*. A
persistent vitality has kept this paper alive thru a
good deal of thick and thin since 1852. In helping to
pay this debt we shall also help to keep open an honorable vocation to colored men who, if they will be printers, must "shinny on their own side." Knowing the
conditions of the masses of our people, no large sums
were asked for; the people were requested to club together and send on a number of little gifts, which might
be at a stated time exhibited and sold at a fair. And
thus the debt liquidated by a co-operative effort would
be an instructive lesson of how light a burden becomes
when borne by the many instead of the few. "Send
something which you yourself have made or produced," we said. "Let what you send be made valuable by your artistic skill, your invention, and your industry." It was hinted that an exhibition of this sort
might be greatly useful and creditable to us as a
people, and that anything, from a potato to a picture,
would be accepted. The result has been such as to
gratify the highest expectations. Responses by donaa-
tions of articles or money have been received from the
following States: Michigan, Wisconsin, Indiana, Illi-
nois, Ohio, Arkansas, Kansas, Texas, Louisiana, Mis-
sissippi, Georgia, North Carolina, South Carolina,
Kentucky, Maryland, Delaware, New Jersey, New

York, Rhode Island, Florida, Massachusetts, Virginia,
Pennsylvania, Indian Territory and the District of
Columbia. About two-thirds of the things at this fair
were sent from the South, from Texas and some other
distant parts, where the expressage on a box would
have been large—our sugar cane cost our Florida
friends $7 to express—from these points the people
sent money; more than $80.00 thus contributed was
spent to buy things on commission to help out. It
seemed due to the people of the South and West who
have so generously sent their little gifts to help keep
alive a printing establishment in this city, from which
there is no hope of their receiving any pecuniary benefit, it seemed due to them, I repeat, that we should not
diminish the profits arising from the sale of these
things by the purchase of gaudy and artistic flummery
to dress the hall; so those who come to visit us will
not, we hope, expect too much. The poor people who
have sent us these things have shown a spirit of self-
denial and of generous zeal which borders on heroism.
All classes, including old people and young children,
have vied with each other in sending some little article
for the fair. If we had dared last year to predict these
wonderful results it would have been set down as
transcendental bosh, but we would have spoken "but
the words of truth and soberness." The different kinds
of needlework, crochet work and worsted work are
very creditable; as also is the model of a church in
Providence, Rhode Island, sent by a little boy; two
ships, full rigged, and especially the decorated plates,

and the pictures, "A Rocky Coast," the "Coast of Maine," and the "Wreck at Cape May" last summer, by H. O. Tanner, son of the editor of *The Christian Recorder*. The last contributors are colored lads, and I venture nothing in saying that their work would be creditable to any exhibition. The well-known artists, Robert Douglass and Wm. H. Dorsey, have many fine paintings on exhibition, especially an oil painting of Mr. Fred Douglass. The agricultural products could have been far larger than they are but for two reasons; first, it was especially understood in the beginning that this exhibition was to show, not what the few can do when they do a great deal, but what the many can do when each does a little; secondly, we were not able to pay the cost of expressage. I mean no reflection in any quarter when I ask thoughtful people if an exhibition of this kind, and for this cause, is not almost as important as holding a convention and reading a lot of "papers." The great lesson to be taught by this fair is the value of co-operative effort to make our cents dollars, and to show us what help there is for ourselves in ourselves. That the colored people of this country have enough money to materially alter their financial condition, was clearly demonstrated by the millions of dollars deposited in the Freedmen's Bank, that they have the good sense, and the unanimity to use this power is now proven by this industrial exhibition and fair. It strikes me that much of the talk about the exodus has proceeded upon the high-handed assumption that, owing largely to the credit system of the South, the colored people there are forced to the alternative to "curse God, and die," or else "go West." Not a bit of it. The people of the South, it is true, cannot produce hundreds of dollars, but they have millions of pennies; and millions of pennies make tens of thousands of dollars. By clubbing together and lumping their pennies, a fund might be raised in the cities of the South that the poorer classes might fall back upon while their crops are growing, or else by the opening of co-operative stores become their own creditors and so effectually rid themselves of their merciless extortioners. "O, they won't do anything; you can't get them united on anything!" The best way for a man to prove that he can do a thing is to do it, and that is what we have done. This fair, participated in by twenty-four States in the Union, and got up for a purpose which is of no pecuniary benefit to those concerned in it, effectually silences all slanders about "we won't or we can't do," and teaches its own instructive and greatly needed lessons of self-help, the best help that any man can have, next to God's.

Those who have this matter in charge have studiously avoided preceding it with noisy and demonstrative babblings, which are so often the vapid precursors of promises as empty as themselves; therefore in some quarters our fair has been overlooked. It is not, we think, a presumptuous interpretation of this great movement, to say that the voice of God now seems to utter, "Speak to the people that they go forward." "Go forward" in what respect? Teach the millions of poor colored laborers of the South how much power they have in themselves, by co-operation of effort, and by a combination of their small means to change the despairing poverty which now drives them from their homes, and makes them a millstone around the neck of any community, South or West. Secondly, that we shall go forward in asking to enter the same employments which other people enter. Within the past ten years we have made almost no advance in getting our youth into industrial and business occupations. It is just as hard to get a boy into a printing office now as it was ten years ago. It is simply astonishing when we consider how many of the common vocations of life colored people are shut out of. Colored men are not admitted to the Printers' Trade Union, nor, with very rare exceptions, are they employed in any city of the United States in a paid capacity as printers or writers, one of the rare exceptions being the employment of H. Price Williams, on the Sunday *Press* of this city. We are not employed as salesmen, or pharmacists, or saleswomen, or bank clerks, or merchants' clerks, or tradesmen, or mechanics, or telegraph operators, or to any degree as State or Government officials, and I could keep on with the string of "ors" until to-morrow morning, but the patience of a reader has its limit.

Slavery made us poor, and its gloomy, malicious shadow tends to keep us so. I beg to say, kind reader, that this is not spoken in a spirit of recrimination; we have no quarrel with our fate, and we leave your

Christianity to yourself. Our faith is firmly fixed in that "Eternal Providence," that in its own good time will "justify the ways of God to man." But, believing that to get the right men into the right places is a "consummation most devoutly to be wished," it is a matter of serious concern to us to see our youth, with just as decided diversity of talent as any other people, all herded together into three or four occupations. It is cruel to make a teacher or a preacher of a man who ought to be a printer or a blacksmith, and that is exactly what we are now obliged to do.. The most advance that has been made since the war has been done by political parties, and it is precisely into political positions that we think it least desirable that our youth should enter. We have our choice of the professions, but, as we have not been endowed with a monopoly of brains, it is not probable that we can contribute to the bar a great lawyer, except once in a great while. The same may be said of medicine; nor are we able to tide over the "starving time," between the reception of a diploma and the time that a man's profession becomes a paying one.

Being determined to know whether this industrial and business ostracism was "in ourselves or in our stars," we have from time to time, knocked, shaken and kicked at these closed doors of work. A cold, metallic voice from within replies, "We do not employ colored people." Ours not to make reply, ours not to question why. Thank heaven, we are not

obliged to do and die, having the preference to do
or die, we naturally prefer to do. But we can not
help wondering if some ignorant or faithless stew-
ard of God's work and God's money hasn't blundered.
It seems necessary that we should make known to the
good men and women who are so solicitous about our
souls and our minds that we haven't quite got rid of
our bodies yet, and until we do we must feed and clothe
them; and this thing of keeping us out of work forces
us back upon charity. That distinguished thinker, Mr.
Henry C. Carey, in his valuable works on Political
Economy, has shown by the truthful and irresistible
logic of history that the elevation of all peoples to a
higher moral and intellectual plane, and to a fuller
investiture of their civil rights has always steadily kept
pace with the improvements in their physical condition. Therefore we feel that resolutely and in unmis-
takable language, yet in the dignity of moderation, we
should strive to make known to all men the justice of
our claims to the same employments as other men
under the same conditions. We do not ask that any
one of our people shall be put into a position because
he is a colored person, but we do most emphatically
ask that he shall not be kept out of a position because
he is a colored person. "An open field and no favors"
is all that is requested. The time was when to put a
colored boy or girl behind a counter would have been
to decrease custom; it would have been a tax upon the
employer, and a charity that we were too proud to

accept; but public sentiment has changed. I am satisfied that the employment of a colored clerk or a colored saleswoman wouldn't even be a "nine days' wonder." It is easy of accomplishment, and yet it is not done. To thoughtless and headstrong people who meet duty with impertinent dictation I do not now address myself; but to those who wish the most gracious of all blessings, a fuller enlightenment as to their duty, to those I beg to say, think of what is said in this appeal.

We do not ask our white friends to come out and make this fair a success. If the word "grand" was not so abominably ill used, I would say that we have already made it a grand success; come and help us make it a greater one. For ten days the colored citizens have crowded this fair. They have bought more than half our contributions. From the ministers of the churches, irrespective of denomination, to the ladies who are attending tables, and the United Order of Masons who rented us the hall, all have shown a generosity, devotion and a warmth of public spirit worthy of the highest praise.

Believing that all efforts at self-help are worthy of respect, and when a man is using every effort in his power to help himself he may with propriety call upon his friends for encouragement, I now respectfully submit this matter to the citizens of Philadelphia and cordially invite them to visit us. As those of us who have charge of the fair are working-women, we do not open it until five o'clock in the afternoon. It is held in Masonic Hall, on Eleventh street, between Pine and Lombard, and will continue all this week.

II.

ELEMENTARY EDUCATION.

Y DEEP interest centers in elementary education for several reasons; first, because it is at this period of the child's life that habits are formed and tastes cultivated which may guide him in the pursuit of knowledge and happiness in after life, and which by the alchemy of experience are to change the elements of what he has learned into wisdom for his highest happiness. All higher learning is but a combination of a few simple elements, and when these are well taught, it clears away the difficulty of future acquisitions, and nature can spread her beauty before eyes that can see and teach the marvelous precision of her laws, to ears that can hear. I call this opening the doors upward and outward, whereas a different way of instruction is like going out of a room backward.

Again, we want to lift education out of the slough of the passive voice. Little Mary goes to school to be educated, and her brother John goes to the high school for the same purpose. It is too often the case that the passive voice has the right of way, whereas in the very beginning we should call into active service all the faculties of mind and body. Unfortunately book learning is so respectable, and there is so much of it all about us, that it is apt to crowd out the prosy process of thinking, comparing, reasoning, to which our wisest efforts should be directed.

Now, when we consider how much is lost by those who lose the benefit of the elementary development, and are therefore unable to pursue the higher branches with any degree of success or comfort to themselves or others, it is evident that this subject is worthy of a wise investigation and we must ask ourselves, how far are we responsible for this condition of affairs? I fear that the reason that so many are unable to keep up when they begin the higher studies is because they never mastered the elementary principles.

If a pupil is absent review day, or demonstration day, he is sure to feel the loss keenly in further pursuit of his studies. Growth in learning and acquisition proceeds slowly and by steps, and we must follow nature's direction.

To be at our business punctually and promptly every day is positively necessary for success, and no trifling excuse ought to be sufficient to keep us from our duty. You know what Uncle Dread said: "Scuses, scuses, the world is built on scuses." A habit of always being on hand in time will save the child from much loss in its after life.

I think a very profitable way to help those who have been absent to make up for what they have lost, while at the same time they are getting the work better understood, is to have daily reviews of at least one half of the lesson; part oral and a part written. Such a course will be beneficial even to those who were not absent. It will be found very profitable always to have two or three divisions of the class. The divisions can be based upon ability to do the work rapidly or slowly. For where a person who is very quick gets beside a person who is very slow, he feels that he is wasting his time and becomes very impatient. And now is the time for the exercise of that Christian courtesy which will help us all the way through life.

Never let the word "dumb" be used in your class, or anything said disrespectful of parents or guardians who may have helped the child. If the teacher has the questions or the review well selected, they can be quickly given out and no one division has to wait for the other. When the teacher has given all the time possible to certain work, the divisions can be stopped, arranged in order and the pupils will profit by the criticisms of one another, the teacher making no corrections that can possibly be made by the class; thus inviting and stimulating the critical knowledge or judgment of all; whether in punctuation, spelling, subject matter, or the appearance of the work; the advanced lesson already having been heard by the teacher.

Blackboards are of great use in schools, and are a mercy to the eyes of the pupils that are thus released from the printed page; or if we can't have blackboards, then we can use brown paper, saved up from bundles containing articles, etc.

I do not see how a teacher can succeed well without ingenuity, because ways of finding means to an end must often be discovered by the teacher. It has been said that not only from the elementary classes, but also from the higher classes, those that drop out do so from the want of better elementary training.

I should like to ask why some of the axioms that might be so helpful are not brought to bear much earlier in the course of instruction. For instance the square of the sum, the square of the difference, and the rectangle of the sum and difference, as

$(5+3)\times(5+3)$, $(5-3)\times(5-3)$ and $(5+3)\times(5-3)$

To do this work and then show by inspection that the first contains

1. Square of the sum.
2. Square of the difference.
3. Rectangle of the sum and difference.

The multiplication table offers a fruitful field for study, developing the tables of 2's, 3's and 4's, etc., and picking out cubes and squares in each one.

I've often had teachers say to me, Oh, that was learned long ago.

The numerical cube is the product of a number taken twice as a factor or multiplied into itself once:

The geometrical square is an equilateral rectangle:

The numerical cube is the product of a number taken three times as a factor or multiplied into itself twice.

The geometrical cube is a solid bounded by six equal squares.

One of the most useful operations is, having a fractional part of a number, to find it; as, 30 is $\frac{5}{7}$ of what number? We shall meet this operation often, even in higher arithmetic, and it can be easily taught when teaching the multiplication table.

Of course, when pupils are just beginning they cannot be left so much to themselves, for everything must be carefully done.

III.

METHODS OF INSTRUCTION.

 AM always sorry to hear that such and such a person is going to school to be educated.

This is a great mistake. If the person is to get the benefit of what we call education, he must educate himself, under the direction of the teacher.

To go into the school and take one's seat is not a favorable sign for the work that is going to be done; the very first thing to do is to get our pupils into an orderly arrangement for working. The teacher probably has two or three divisions; one set will be employed at the blackboard, and one will recite to the teacher the lesson of the day. The work at the blackboard is review work. And just here is a very important step.

What shall the review consist of? I would say let one-half or three-fourths of the lesson be the review, and spend the rest of the time on the advanced lesson; that is, the lesson for the day. In order that no time may be lost in giving out the review, the teacher will have all the points selected for review written off, and some member of the class may pass these papers round to the division that has the review, and each one as he takes his paper goes to the board to do his work; or, if he has no board, then he must have the paper to write on, but let us hope that a very few will have to use paper, for the eye needs rest from the small writing with the pencil, and the eye of the teacher is also benefited by not having to scrutinize small letters, whereas the chalk on the blackboard sets off the words and is a great relief to the eye.

When the teacher has given as much time as he can with the work on the board, he stops the class that has been reciting to him and both divisions undertake the corrections of the board work; this must be done in a systematic manner.

Where shall we begin?

I should say to begin with what appears to be the poorest work on the board, in order that the most corrections may be made, and now the teacher must show great skill in keeping the attention of the class fixed upon one matter, for when they are enthusiastic, all will want to speak at once, or some will want to make remarks, or to jump from one point to another before the first is completely done.

Those who have been absent from time to time will find the reviews a great benefit to them, for when there is a distinct failure, we often hear the person say, I was absent when that lesson was given, for I don't remember it at all. How, then, could these children go on with the advanced lesson with any degree of understanding or profit?

Trial examinations upon simple principles that have been given for some time will oftentimes be of great profit to the class.

The teacher is not supposed to be talking or looking out of the window while the examination goes on, but is passing quietly from seat to seat looking at each person's work, so that when the time is up he is quite well informed as to how each person has succeeded in the work required of him, and what the principal errors are.

The vital errors are errors in the principles used. The misspelled words, grammatical errors, and anything else wrong comes in for its share of correction.

This correction by the teacher, coming immediately after the work is done, is very helpful to those being examined, and saves the teacher from carrying the work home and having to go over it all by himself, and besides, the pupils get far more benefit from this co-operative correction, as it may be called.

In order that the teacher may do his best work while his class is with him, it is necessary that he should have his work all arranged in his own mind before he meets the class. If the teacher is ingenious and he cannot be a good teacher without ingenuity, he can think out many helpful ways to occupy his pupils to the best advantage while he is with them. The lowest classes, as well as the highest, will reap great benefit from this skillful arrangement of their work by their teacher. I have before spoken of division of classes into two or three sections, but the teacher who makes the division must be very careful not to say of number one, this is the slowest division; or of another, this one can go more rapidly.

The teacher knows upon what principle to form his division, but if he begins to state his reasons to the class he will find it like throwing down the apple of discord: there will be no end to the exclamations of those who are in number two, who say that they could go on with number three, and those in number one will declare they can work just as fast as number two.

It is enough for the teacher to say that the classes can be managed and can do far more work when the teacher handles them in smaller numbers, so that one division can be writing while another is reciting, and all are kept busy as bees. The whole class should be working under the eye of the teacher. It ought not be necessary for the teacher to turn around to see if those who are at the board or those who are doing the work in their seats are in good order and not disturbing one another. A skillful arrangement on the part of the teacher can bring the whole under his own supervision. But the teacher should by no means take up a position as if watching the pupils. Put their conduct on high ground at the very beginning, and when they disappoint you by doing what the teacher would object to, we must let them know how disappointed we are by such a betrayal of trust, and they may start the next day to do better; and so, little by little, these young people will acquire the habit of doing what they know is right, whether the teacher sees them or not.

I have before spoken of talking in classes, because it disturbs the teacher and disturbs the class, but I have often heard them say, suppose I only whisper, would that disturb the class? As far as my experience goes, there can be no compromise with talking or whispering while the work is going on. The habit of self control is not easily acquired, but when the pupil has his tongue under control St. James says, "He is able also to bridle the whole body." I believe that many a dreadful result has followed a too free use of the tongue, for it is well said, one word always brings on another and before we know it we are in the midst of a hot dispute over something. Not only the children, but the teacher may have too nimble a tongue, and may use it, not to explain what is difficult to the pupils, but to discuss why they are so stupid as to need any explanation.

Sometimes the teachers make uncomplimentary remarks about those who need to have the matter explained, saying, anybody could see that. I heard of a little boy once whose father had worked out some examples for him in arithmetic. The teacher should have known that the child did not do the work, and should have been careful about speaking of that work.

"Why, that's a very old-fashioned way of doing that work; we don't do that way now," and other things were said even more uncomplimentary of the person who did the work for the child. Here, again, is a case where the teacher needs to be corrected. It may as well be understood that all remarks which are disrespectful to the parents or guardian ought never to be indulged in by the teacher. Calling names, the words stupid, or dunce, or dumb, serves only to make the pupil angry or to discourage him. Here, again, the teacher ought to think of himself when he was taking his first lessons. Whenever a pupil has spoken disrespectfully to a teacher and the teacher can say with truth, do I not always speak kindly and politely to you? the case is won without any more argument. I have never known this to fail. I have often seen a tear steal down the face of a child, and then I neither asked for an apology nor forced one, but of the child's own volition it came at once.

How can we get the child trained to do what he dislikes to do and to obey our laws without corporal punishment? If the parent begins early enough, there is every hope of success, but, unfortunately, it is thought the child isn't old enough to understand what we wish him to do. For instance, a mother sees her little boy going around the room with a hammer, and of course looking for something to hit with it. She repeatedly tells him to bring the hammer to mamma, but he pays no attention to it. And, waiting a little while, she goes to him and takes the hammer away from him. He struggles with all his little might to keep it.

The mother should know it will not be very long before that little fellow will be strong enough, not only to keep the hammer, but to do with it as he will. Then was the time, when he paid no attention, for her to have taught that child to obey her and bring her the hammer of his own will. A little battle like that lost or won means victory or defeat for that child's future character.

To learn to give up his own will to that of his parents or teacher, as we must to the Great Teacher of all, will surely make us happy in this life and in the life to come. Happy is the child who has wise parents and guardians, and whose training is continued when he enters the school room. Whereas when a child has had little training in obedience at home it is not long before he gets into trouble in the school room, for there he finds himself surrounded by laws which he must obey if he makes the progress in his studies and in his character which he ought to make, which will give him an honored place in the school and out of it.

IV.

DIAGNOSIS AND DISCIPLINE.

T IS possible for the teacher to notice who those are in the class who do not care for learning what we have to give them; and the question to ask ourselves is, Why? Are the lessons too hard? or are they too long? Is the child well? Above all, does he seem to pass from one to another part of study with ease and comfort to himself, or is he troubled and uncertain? Does he often give excuses for staying away, and does he fail to get the meaning of what we are trying to teach him? When he fails in his lessons, does the teacher let the parent or guardian know, and how is this information supposed to be received at his home?

I have heard of a case where whenever the child failed in his lessons, word was sent to his father, who gave him no dinner and locked him up in the cellar. Would this punishment incline the child to love his studies or to get them any better? On the contrary, would he not hate them and be glad when he is through with them? We should remember that punishments that do not correct, harden. For this reason we should try to find out what the real trouble is, and then what will best make up for it.

Examinations privately conducted without letting the person know what you are looking for may give the true source of the trouble. And we may discover why the work we have given is not done. For instance, at one time being accused of having promoted a scholar to a higher class who could not multiply, I replied, "I know he can multiply." "Try him yourself," said the teacher. And I did try him myself, and found that when the multiplier and the multiplicand were separated as in long division the child did not know at what end to begin to multiply. As soon as I let in light on this point he went ahead like everything. Sometimes I've said to myself as I've watched the way that a pupil worked, you say you cannot get this example; no, and you never would have gotten it if you had kept on that way. All learning proceeds by steps. And the absences of pupils may be illustrated by a ladder with a rung out here and there. So that instead of the person going up easily and smoothly, he is every now and then distracted by the difficulty of the step. Let the pupils make a ladder, and show these parts out. Every succeeding lesson is carefully planned by a preceding demonstration or piece of instruction, and when a pupil is absent on one of these days it is very difficult to make up for it. We ought to be very careful about apportioning any severe punishment, and it would be well to sleep over it before we decide.

If the teacher is just as angry as the pupil, which is sometimes the case, he is not apt to do the wisest and kindest thing to bring about a spirit of repentance and a wish to correct what has been wrong. Happy is the teacher who can wait to win his pupil, to what he believes to be right.

I can think of no agency in the formation of a beautiful character that is more powerful than the daily correction and training which we call discipline, and here the teacher is all powerful.

The child can read his books and get much information from them to help him in his education, but he cannot see when he should be corrected, nor how to do so. To be apt in diagnosing a case to find the difficulties that a child labors under, and as apt in the correcting discipline, are valuable qualifications for a teacher. These qualifications cannot be put down in a book to be learned as ordinary lessons. We can only give suggestions, and the teacher must work out his own plans, and acquire the knowledge by actual practice.

Many a child called dull, would advance rapidly under a patient, wise and skillful teacher, and the teacher should be as conscientious in the endeavor to improve himself as he is to improve the child.

V.

OBJECT OF PUNISHMENT.

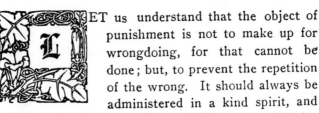ET us understand that the object of punishment is not to make up for wrongdoing, for that cannot be done; but, to prevent the repetition of the wrong. It should always be administered in a kind spirit, and should be so reasonable, that a child's sense of justice would agree with it. He should see that if he repeated the wrong act it would not be good for him nor for the teacher nor his parents nor the school.

Of course no cruel punishment should ever be allowed, and if whipping is to be done it is far better for the parent to do it, for his hand is restrained by love.

I once heard this story. Two little boys were out selling matches; one having sold out met a comrade who had not sold any. Said the one who had been successful to his comrade, "I will take your matches and give you my money. If I am not sold out when I get home I shall get a whipping like yourself. Your master would whip you, but my father would whip me, but he wouldn't whip so hard nor so long as your master." A page of philosophy could not give us a better understanding of the case, than is given by the incident of these two little match boys.

Habits of obedience can be taught to a child when it is little so that little by little he learns to give up his own will to that of his parents or teacher, which alone can make us happy in this life and the life to come. When spoken to disrespectfully I would say to the child, "Do I not always speak to you kindly and politely?" I never had to make any other argument. I never asked for any apology, and I never failed to get it. Not perhaps at that time, but after it had been thought of. It seems to me that it would be very unwise to send a bad report to the parent concerning the child unless we know the disposition of the parent and his means of correcting. This is very important, for if the child is not corrected of his fault, he is apt to become worse instead of better.

Never be in a hurry about punishing a child. Think well over it first. Always investigate a case thoroughly before you punish a child.

Try never to whip the child yourself; always report the child to the parents when such correction is necessary.

Never deprive a child of all of his recess. He is not a block of wood; he needs fresh air and water and he will not be in a condition to recite unless he has time for that. Some teachers think they haven't punished enough unless they have taken all of his recess. This is a great mistake. To take a child's lunch from him is a great mistake. There is no use in attempting to teach a hungry child.

The ventilation of the school room may be responsible for what we call stupidity on the part of the child.

Let a stream of oxygen pass through the room and what a waking-up there will be! Sometimes if a child is naughty it will do him good to run out in the yard a minute.

Remember all the time you are dealing with a human being, whose needs are like your own.

A child knows well when a teacher is kind and considerate of him.

Never take away a child's occupation as a punishment.

The secret of good government is occupation of the right kind.

Keep your pupils pleasant by occupying them with your work and they will not be apt so to give you trouble. There are a number of devices called "Busy Work for the School Room." These little occupations are suited to every grade, and the teacher should make a study of them and have them at his command. The teacher knows who the restive pupils are, and work for these should be prepared beforehand. A great deal of what we call mischief is animal activity on the part of the child, and we must use that activity to make the child do our work and not his.

There is too much repression and suppression in schools.

Let the child do something of himself and see what he will do. The teacher must prepare for his work before he goes into the school by getting together as much simple apparatus as possible, and finding means of illustration.

There are certain kinds of punishments that should never be resorted to, such as shutting a child up in the school house while you go to your dinner, or shutting him up in a dark closet and keeping him there longer than a half hour, or boxing his ears or hitting him over the head or calling him names.

Try kindness; try to find the wiser way for correcting the wrong.

Be careful of arousing a spirit of revenge in your pupils.

VI.

MORAL INSTRUCTION.

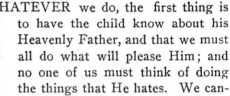HATEVER we do, the first thing is to have the child know about his Heavenly Father, and that we must all do what will please Him; and no one of us must think of doing the things that He hates. We cannot grow straight and beautiful if we disobey His laws: and so, we must preoccupy the ground very early, for evil is so crafty that even with all our vigilance it will get its work in somewhere. "Didst not thou sow good seed in thy field? whence then hath it tares?"

However brilliant a person may be intellectually, however skillful in the arts and sciences, he must be reliable; he must be trustworthy.

We must know that we can depend upon his word. Obedience, truthfulness, love of right, and sincerity, must be instilled and inculcated by precept and by example, but always in kindness.

Love wins when everything else will fail. You say that your child resists all your efforts to break him of his bad habits and make him become good. Have you tried kindness? Have you tried love?

The Commandments in verse are very easily learned; therefore I would have them taught.

Thou should have no other Gods before me.
Before no idol bend thy knee.
Take not the name of God in vain.
Nor dare the Sabbath Day profane.
Give both thy parents honor due.
Take heed that thou no murder do.
Abstain from words and deeds unclean.
Nor steal though thou art poor and mean.
Nor make a willful lie and love it.
What is thy neighbors do not covet.
With all thy heart love God above,
And as thyself thy neighbor love.

The pieces so called which the child learns, will have much to do with forming his mind, and so we pick them out with a great deal of care.

Love to father and mother, sister and brother; love to home and country; love to animals.

In short fill the mind with what we know will keep it pure and beautiful. Above all things see that the child is getting a love to take in and do what is taught him. Scripture that the child can understand will of course be our first ally, as, "Jesus loves me this I know, for the Bible tells me so."

Bands of Hope must be kept in view, for in the very beginning the child must be taught the danger of strong drink. The selection of pieces to sing must be observed with great care. However pretty a tune is, if it doesn't carry beautiful words we should not choose it.

The books which our children read should also be carefully looked into. We should do well always in Christmas times and other times to be sure that one of the presents is a book. And the child should be encouraged to make his own little library case by utilizing a starch or soap box. Ingenious young people can soon make a very presentable library case.

Studies in history, American, English, French, etc., natural history and poetry, which children love so much, can also be among the books.

Happy are the children whose parents know the importance of teaching them to love and care for books while they are young. Among the little societies in our school, there was one for charitable purposes and entirely in the hands of the children. Each one was invited, not forced, to give one cent a week. This sum amounted to $75 or $100 a year.

They took charge of small cases of want and destitution until they could report them to the proper societies. And it was a great comfort to me when the time came to make their contributions to various charities, such as the Children's Home; the Aged Home; Society for the Prevention of Cruelty to Animals, and other charities; and to see them making out their little checks was also comforting. There was much merriment when we came to this little business, for how to draw up a money order, or how to make out a check and other little matters of bookkeeping had to be taught.

As I have said; nobody was obliged to give the

penny a week, but they all were invited to do so. When the young people came home after vacation, they had made sums to help themselves along, and those sums added together varied from $2,000 to $2,500.

Of course the students in the higher classes made most, because they could get more responsible work to do. Very interesting incidents cropped out during these reports, but I can only mention one or two. One of our little girls between eleven years and twelve went along as chore girl. But there was consternation in the household when it was discovered that the cook had disappointed. "But," said the little girl, "I can cook." So it was only necessary to change places. And our little girl found her wages increased from $1 to $3 a week.

Another case of a little girl only about seven years who had saved up a little something during the vacation. "Now what did you do?" said I, "I know you couldn't have worked." "I used to go every Sunday and take a blind lady to church. Then she used to give me fifty cents every time I went and I saved it up."

Many incidents might be told of this kind, but I am warned that printing costs money, but the training which bears fruit in a thoughtful application of what we have learned deserves encouragement.

There is, in my opinion, no incompatibility between higher learning and work.

The study room and the workshop ought to have their hours so arranged that both can be advanced together. The saw and the plane waiting with gracious patience upon the hammer and the anvil, and both accompaniments.

A skillful arrangement of the hours of study and of demonstration will prove the workableness of what I am saying, and ten years hence, when that same carpenter or blacksmith may be wanted to give his opinion on some knotty points in interdependent study which men's reasoning has failed to smooth off, it may be found that our mechanic may have need for the learning which was not thought necessary when he was getting his trade.

Trustworthiness and reliability should be the outgrowth of the moral instruction which we give. Without this fine fruit of all our teaching, all else will be of little account. I might have said of no account.

VII.

GOOD MANNERS.

HE teaching of good manners in the home, is of the highest importance. The little child is taught to say, if you please, and thank you, not only to mother and father, but to brothers and sisters; and I know of nothing that conduces more to the happiness of the home than the manner of speaking to each other by all the members of the family. Some people seem to think that good manners need only be exercised toward our superiors or toward strangers, but this is a great mistake. A gentleman can always be told by the way he speaks to those that he thinks are his inferiors in some respect. His equals he does not wish to offend, his superiors he does not dare to offend, and of those whom he considers his inferiors he would be all the more considerate.

It is a very unsafe thing to graduate our politeness to what we suppose to be the position of the person we are addressing. I have heard of a car conductor who was very impolite to an old gentleman on his train because he was rather shabbily dressed; and he made many inquiries as to how he came by his rate book, with other unnecessary questions, which did not concern him. A short time after, when he was released from his position, he was astonished to find that he had been talking to the president of the road. Good manners will often take people where neither money nor education will take them.

If we could follow many serious evils in life to their sources, we should find that many of them sprang from what we should regard as very insignificant matters. The girl who could not hold her tongue in school, but was always ready with a smart reply, may trace her broken household some day to that same fluency in speech. For it is indeed true that one word brings on another and the word that is brought on is generally not such as to help matters. We do well to remember that a soft answer turneth away wrath, but grievous words stir up anger. Words, words, how they can make or mar our lives! The temper must be curbed, must be held in if necessary with "bit and bridle" until it yields to control.

VIII.

HOW TO TEACH READING AND SPELLING.

HERE are now so many new ways of teaching reading and spelling that teachers can have their choice and take whatever plan they find the most effective.

To learn to read, write and spell one word the first day, will be found to be very interesting to the children. The word "man" is a good word to begin with, because day after day by the addition of one more letter each day we can form a sentence. Words are more interesting than letters, and sentences are more interesting than words. So that as soon as possible the teacher wants to make a sentence. But it is not supposed that we should omit to teach the alphabet in order, for we know that this is necessary. But by no means allow this to be done mentally. Have the book or the chart with the letters large and distinctly made, and have the children's eyes follow the work as the teacher points to each letter and calls its name. There are many little devices that a teacher can use to get the children interested in the work. Among them may be picking out the printed letters that they have learned when

5

they see them in a book or paper, and sometimes the teacher will have them in a little box and the children are asked to pick out such and such a letter and bring it to the teacher. The movements of the hand and arm in making letters should be frequently practiced by the pupils, and this is a wonderful help when they come to make the letters on the board or on the paper.

The pupils are thus led along skillfully until they are ready to take the first lessons in their readers; then, how the work will jump! No drawling tones will be heard then, for their preparations will make them feel that they know the whole book. The articles *a* and *the* having been pronounced naturally as "ăh," "thĕ," the child will read, "Thĕ boy has ă dog." And not, "The boy has ā dog. Sometimes it is very hard to break up this unnatural way of reading. As the child's writing has kept pace with its reading, one child can copy a letter on the board while the teacher hears the others read. When the writing is finished, the whole class turns to the board to correct whatever has been written, and then they have a lively time. From lesson to lesson this plan is pursued until the child gets through with the Third Reader, and then what a mass of information the child has acquired, and what facility in reading, writing and spelling! But there can hardly be a better way to train a child to think and to reason than by the constant comparisons which he has had to make use of in learning the letters and all about them, Besides,

when a person can read, the whole realm of knowledge
lies open before him, and if necessary he can go on
by himself; for many a learned person had to begin
in this way. I will next speak of advanced reading.
A clear-cut enunciation of the vowels, the consonants
and certain combinations of consonants have been insisted upon during the elementary stages of the child's
progress. Nor has he been allowed to drop his final
t's or *d's* nor to say *w* for *v*. Fortunate is the child
who has had a careful and well-prepared teacher in
his early lessons in reading. Before the child begins
to read he should know the definitions of the words
he is using, and this matter too has had attention in
the preceding reading lessons. It would be a great
pity to allow the child to consider a lesson learned,
simply because he could pronounce the words fluently,
for the meaning is all-important. It is very helpful if
the definitions of the words in the reading lessons
are written at the top of the page as they are in
some books; and the preparation for the day's lesson
should be to have these words correctly pronounced,
and their definitions written upon the board, and as
words have more than one definition, it is good practice to see what other meanings the class can give.
When the class begins to read, let the pupils read
the lesson straight thru, going from one to the
other without interruption. If any one has been looking off his book and is not ready, pass him by and go
right on to the next one. Do not stop to correct mis-
pronounced words, but wait until the lesson has been

read thru once.   In this way we shall get the sense of the lesson.   It is objected that if we leave the corrections until the reading is finished, they will be forgotten; but stopping after each one reads, to say what you noticed was wrong, etc., keeps the pupils from getting a connected idea of the lesson, and hence, destroys the interest in it.   When the lesson is read thru again the corrections are made.   The spelling lesson should consist largely of words taken from the reading lesson, for these will be the most useful that the pupil can have, and when these words are recited, it should be by writing them in sentences.   It may be objected that this takes too much time, as the time given to spelling is generally less than that given to other subjects.   But are not reading and spelling the most important lessons that the child can have? Five words correctly defined and written in sentences are of more value than twenty words simply spelled correctly.   In the very beginning the marks of punctuation should be used, and the marks of contraction and the possessive case should be observed closely, as, John's father was *too* busy *to* waste *two* minutes from his business.   The architect *planned* the building and the carpenter *planed* some of the joists the next day.

"I do not complain of the boys' work," said their father, "but I wished they had gone farther while they were about it."

Men's and women's clothing is made from different kinds of cloth.   It will be seen that the teacher takes advantage of simple grammatical rules to have the writing correctly done. I will hereafter give a number of sentences to illustrate what I mean. I should have said, that as soon as possible, the child should be taught to write a letter. The words mother, father, sister, brother and teacher should be spelled and written for him so that the little letter beginning Dear mother can begin to be made the subject of instruction.

The child's interest is awakened and he will try his best to learn other words that he will write to his mother. If this begins in the first reader, before the third is finished the child will be quite a little scribe. But we must proceed very slowly with this work. One or two words at a time are all that can be taken, and for this reason, very careful training is necessary on the part of the teacher. If the child gets thoroughly interested in his lessons, it will certainly stop the truancies. It is well worth while to let the child see how he is getting ahead. The English language is certainly not an easy one to learn, and much patience is required to learn to use it correctly; but a thoughtful teacher can by pointing out differences help the pupil to remember the many points necessary in correct reading and spelling

Dictation exercises should begin with the First Reader, and follow all thru the course in reading. It is very unfortunate that reading in schools should be stopped so soon. If a child can pronounce certain words correctly, and especially if he has gone thru the Fourth Reader, it is supposed that he doesn't need any more instruction in reading, but immediately passes into what are considered more difficult subjects.

This is the reason that more pupils do not acquire a taste for reading, because as soon as they get thru the task of pronouncing words and are just ready to enter upon the delightful task of reading by sight, they are supposed to have finished, and the work stops. Whereas, the pupil is just ready to get the thoughts of others in an easy and intelligent way, and he can learn the thoughts of the very best writers the world has ever seen. And before he knows it they become a part of himself, leading him onward and heavenward. Just as when a person has mastered the scales and exercises on the piano, he is not considered to have finished the course in music, but to be in a position to be introduced to the works of the great masters. After hearing a master of the instrument play "Home, Sweet Home" we make up our minds that we never heard it before, and we never did. This matter of reading is far more important than many of us think, because as I have said, it is to continue all our lives long. A first-class reader may be called an elocutionist, because he makes the thoughts of the writer live again in the minds of those who hear. In the very beginning, the child's eyes are trained to recognize the period and comma when he sees them, and to use them correctly when he is writing. The other marks of punctuation come in for their share of attention when he is able to understand them. But besides training the eye, we should remember that the ear should be trained. Read a short sentence to the class and see who can repeat it correctly; you will be astonished to see how few can reproduce the sentence just as it was given. It is no wonder that our Lord said, "Take heed how ye hear."

A distinguished teacher of a high school used to try his entering classes, to see if they were prepared to take down correctly the lectures which they were to receive, and he was astonished to find how differently a simple sentence would be written by them. The teacher can try his class himself by asking them to write down any simple sentence which he may give them. Disputes, nay quarrels, oftentimes are produced because one person says I understood him to say so and so, and another one says I did not understand it that way. If each of these persons should write down what he thought was said, the difference in the way they had heard would soon be evident. Now, as lectures and sermons are given by hearing, how necessary it is that the ear should be trained to repeat correctly the sounds which fall upon it, and this is another reason why the sounds of the letters should be distinctly practiced by speakers and hearers, for there is a great difference in the way people pronounce their words, and some of them it is difficult to understand. We must be careful that the final *d's* and *t's*, *st* and *st's* should be carefully uttered: *v* and *w* are made by different positions of the lips and the vocal organs should be practiced to show how they are to be correctly uttered. As for *r* it is rarely pronounced correctly, and the same may be said of *th* following an *s*, or *c* as, passeth, ceaseth, rejoiceth. In further writing, I will put down the difficult consonant combinations. If a child has an impediment in his speech, the teacher must be very careful about forcing him to read by himself before he has got over the worst of his difficulties. By no means make him an object of fun to the class, nor allow any pupil to make fun of him with his peculiarities when the class is over.

If the class has five times to read during the week, I would take one of these times for recitations. After reciting, let the pieces be written on the board, and here the eye can correct whatever the ear gave wrong. Misspelled words, misplaced capitals, and whatever else needs correction comes under the teacher's eyes, and is written correctly.

Great care should be taken in making the selections for the children to learn. However short the piece may be, it should include some moral principle, or something of beauty in nature or art; but always something that the pupil can understand. Pieces for the different grades are now selected for the teacher, and this makes it easier to find wise selections. But I would be very careful about the funny pieces, for we should teach nothing but what inculcates some pretty thought.

Obedience to our Heavenly Father; love to par-

ents, brothers and sisters; love to country, and kindness to dumb animals; and many other selections
which will hereafter be given. Children learn poetry
far more quickly than they do prose, and so we se-
lect what we teach them largely from poets.

There is a world of happy thoughts all about us,
and if we make wise selections in teaching, they are
quite sure to be remembered. And the grain of truth
which they contain is as encouraging in bringing
forth fruit, as is the grain of mustard seed. What we
sow we reap, and there is no field more fertile than
that of a child's mind. If we plant tomatoes, we get
tomatoes; we certainly should not expect to find
potatoes. And so, if we plant beautiful thoughts and
beautiful words in the child's mind, we shall certainly get the same. But I do not forget the parable
of the tares of the field, for whatever we do, there
is always an active enemy who is doing his sowing
at the same time, and for this reason we must humble
ourselves and pray that the Lord of the Harvest may
protect our child's mind from the sower of evil; for
in spite of all you may do, you will find things in that
child's mind which you never taught him, and which
you cannot account for.

Teaching spelling by dictation exercises is the
most profitable way to get the child to learn what
might otherwise be dry and uninteresting.

Facility in writing to dictation will train the ear
to receive sounds correctly and this is very important.
How often do we hear people say, "but that is not

what I thought was said," and so we have a large class of persons of whom it may be said, "Having ears they hear not, neither do they understand."

The distinct utterance of the vocal elements must be insisted upon, and those elements in their difficult combinations which I have already mentioned.

Sermons, lectures, and much of the instruction which we receive must depend upon the ear for its faithful reproduction. A professor giving a lecture at one time to a number of students of different grades of instruction saw a little boy industriously taking notes, and he asked one of the teachers to let him have the child's paper when he was through.

This was done, and he made the exclamation as he glanced over the notes, "This is wonderful." Then followed the questions. In what class is this child and who is his teacher?

It is evident if the teacher corrects each dictation exercise individually the other pupils will lack the valuable practice which would follow looking over many papers themselves; therefore having exchanged papers each one is called upon for the correction of what he sees wrong on the paper which he has, and the correct form is written on the board. It is also very useful for pupils to learn to read the handwriting of different persons.

I have been asked if I approved teaching the rules of spelling; not all of them by any means, because the pupil can easily learn the rules by his own practice. But the rule for monosyllables and words accented on the last syllable should be thoroughly learned, because it is so frequently applied, as it refers to the formation of so many words in the English language.

About sixty per cent. of our words are old English or Anglo-Saxon.

Thirty per cent. are latin, five per cent. are Greek, and five per cent. words taken from many other languages. Nearly all the monosyllables in the language are old English and are very plain words, and most easily understood. The pronouns, the conjunctions, and nearly all the prepositions are old English, and words of one syllable as we know are old English. These form a sturdy stock like the people that first used them. The Bible, Shakespeare and Bunyan's "Pilgrim's Progress" abound in these words.

They are strong and easy to be understood, whereas the Latin words and the Greek are formed of many syllables, and express different shades of thought and of mental states and action. I suppose these are the "words of learned length and thundering sound, which amazed the gaping rustics gathered round," and made the schoolmaster so famous.

Scientific words are written in the Greek language.

Always avoid using what are called big words when writing on any topic, for they often do nothing but "Darken counsel by words without knowledge." Whereas the duty of the speaker or writer is to get before his hearers or his readers as clear an idea of his thoughts as he can.

Now I am advocating a careful and thorough teaching of spelling, if it is taught by dictation exercises, with a clear knowledge of the use of words, whether it is in the elementary school or the high school, because such instructions are immensely valuable to pupils in all their writings.

The printer at his desk or the writer for the paper, or lawyer in his briefs, or the orator in his pleadings, will be thankful for their thorough knowledge of words and their uses. As the pupils advance in their lessons, it will be a very good thing to have many little essays written on the power of words to bless or destroy, and on the responsibility of those who use them, for, "By thy words thou shalt be justified, and by thy words thou shalt be condemned." Again it has been said, "A wholesome tongue is a tree of life." Let us therefore guard the tongue with wise vigilance, and those whom we teach must be inspired to think about the different effect of kind words and unkind words, therefore to think before they use them. Many a quarrel which has ended even in death started from one bitter word. Many cases could be mentioned which would help to make us more thoughtful and careful in our speech. The pupils must notice the kind of words which are used by the best writers in the books which they are studying, and in the extracts from the best English writers which we are supposed to give them in their weekly lessons. In a school in Africa I found our little children studying the story of Hiawatha, and just as those who have to live upon coarse food may show its effects in their body, so those whose minds are fed upon pure food thought, whether of Longfellow or Whittier or any other first-class poet, will soon show in their spiritual development what they have been studying. "Upon what meat hath this our Caesar fed that he hath grown so great." Can we not see the wisdom of that question and look out for the mental food upon which our children are feeding?

There ought to be a censorship of the press in America, that books that give foolish, unreal or evil ideas of life should never be printed nor reach the eyes of our children. The so-called yellow literature must be offset until it is scouted out of the land by forming the taste for what is pure and good and true in the youth.

Fairy stories, the child delights in, and we must see that what we give them is not too heavy for their young minds.

Hans Christian Anderson has a grain of truth in every one of his stories, and let us see to it that the child has that in other stories which will build up strong moral fibre and encourage him to love the truth. This shows why the teacher should be well-prepared for all classes, but especially for the lower classes, because for them he must supply such reading as he knows will be profitable in the child's daily life. For the kind of reading which is given should be equal to little classics which he will probably remember all his life long, and his taste being thus

slowly formed for what is purest and best in literature, will reject what is foolish and inferior.

The teacher will thus be sending a pure stream
to form that "Well of English undefiled," which in
the future will become a source of purer happiness
than that which can be found in the stories of many
brilliant writers.

IX.

HOW TO TEACH GRAMMAR.

T IS not necessary to wait until children can learn rules of grammatical construction before we teach them how to speak correctly. For be it known that children do not speak according to rules, but according to what they hear.

It will be observed that those who associate with persons who use incorrect grammar will be very apt to fall into the same habit themselves, while those who associate with persons who speak correctly will be found to speak also correctly without any instruction; and in this way you can often tell the kind of associates that one is accustomed to have.

It is for this reason that it is much easier to learn to speak German in Germany, or to speak French in France, than in a country where all the sounds you hear are those of the English language. For this reason, too, teachers of German or French should speak to their pupils in those languages, and not be satisfied with simply reading it to them.

Those who are able to have a German and French nurse for their children will find that the child will speak German to the German nurse and French to the French nurse without difficulty; this ought to teach us something about how languages are acquired.

To speak a language correctly, and also to write it correctly, are of the first importance. Therefore, at the beginning we simply correct what is incorrect in the child's speech, and do not square it by the rules of grammar until he is able to understand it.

We know the grammatical rules which are most likely to be violated, such as singular verbs with plural subjects, and vice versa; as, "Mary and Jane has not finished their lessons yet"; or, "I has no more time to give to the subject."

Another common error is the past tense of the verb for the past participle, as, "I seen him when he done it, and I haven't saw him since."

A child should immediately be corrected when heard to say: "Is you going to the fair?" "I would have went had I been invited."

Why should a child be allowed to say: It is me, it is him, it is her, and not be corrected? Or, I didn't do nothing on my work today; or, I written to my mother yesterday. Such errors are passed unnoticed in children, when that is the very time when corrections should be made and can be made most effectively.

The only way to teach them to write correctly is to have them write. A good rule would be to have them write a little essay once a week, and have it corrected, seeing that all the rules of grammatical construction are properly observed. See that you do not have a **singular pronoun** represented by a **plural antecedent,** as, "let every one attend to their own affairs."

The classes of **pronouns,** being difficult to learn, should be given at an early stage of the child's progress.

There are four classes of pronouns—**personal, relative, interrogative** and **adjective.**

The **adjective pronouns** are themselves divided into four classes, and it will help the child to remember them by a little device like this, pidd, viz.: personal— my hat, her hand, his ball; indefinite—none, any, all, whole, some; demonstrative—this, that—with the plurals—these, those; distributives—each, every, either, neither.

Personal pronouns are those which show by their forms what *person* is meant; I, thou, you, he, she, and it. They are declined: nominative, I; possessive, my or mine; objective, me. Plural, nominative, we; possessive, our or ours; objective, us.

Second person—Nominative, thou; possessive, thy or thine; objective thee; plural, nominative, you; possessive, your or yours; objective, your.

Third person—Nominative, it; possessive, its; objective, it. Plural, nominative, they; possessive, their or theirs; objective, them.

Relative pronouns—Nominative, who; possessive, whose; objective, whom; there is no difference for the plural.

6

Interrogatives who, which and what, are not declined at all.

Compound pronouns are formed by adding "self," viz.: myself, himself, themselves, etc. Ever and soever, added to the relative who, gives it an indefinite force, as, whoever sins, must suffer; whosoever will, let him come.

With respect to the parts of speech, we may say that anything we can see or think of is a **noun**; as, house, goodness. Any word that we can say something with—make a statement, is a **verb**. I can say I run, but cannot say I house.

Conjunctions are the joining words, and with a number of these on hand, we can begin to make up sentences. John *and* James can go, *but* Mary must help her mother, *unless* she does not need her. James is *as* helpful *as* John, *but* Thomas works faster *than* either of them.

Prepositions always govern the objective case, therefore the child must not be allowed to say, between I and you; nor, between you and I, for between you and me.

Teaching the **verb** is very interesting. The attributes, viz.: **voice, mood, tense, number** and **person**, are not equally difficult. For instance, we know what **person** and **number** the **verb** is by the **person** and **number** of its subject, for they must agree.

We can think of three divisions of **time** or **tense**; as, I write today, I wrote yesterday, I shall write tomorrow.

There are three more **tenses**, called **perfect**, or finished: I have written today, I had written when I saw you, and I shall have written before I see you again.

When a past act happens before some other, which is also passed, we call it the **past perfect**; as, I had written the letter before the man called for it.

When a future act happens before some other which is also future, we call it **future perfect**; as, I shall have finished the dress before the lady will call for it. So much for tense.

Now, as to **voice.** We mean that form of the **verb** which shows whether the subject acts, or is acted upon; as, John made the table; or, the table was made by John. Here the child can be shown that only verbs which have an object in the active can be put in the passive form, for the action passes over from the subject to the object; hence the word **transitive** for the **verb,** which simply means going across. When the **verb** has no object, it is called **intransitive;** as, the baby sleeps, the mother lies down for a little rest.

Neuter, when referring to **verbs,** means that the subject neither acts nor is acted upon, and here comes in the use of the verb to be—that is to say—to exist; as, Jane **is** my sister, those boys **are** occupied. It is by means of this great verb to be, that we can put any other verb in the passive voice, or show an act continuing; as, the road **was** constructed by the engineer, the work **is** finished: the cattle **are** fed. Hence, to put a verb in the passive voice, we conjugate the verb to be, **and** write after all its moods and tenses the past participle of the verb; as, I am, I was, I shall be; I have been, I had been, I shall have been. I may, can, or must be; might, could, would or should be; I may, can or must have been; I might, could, would or should have been; to be, to have been; being, been and having been. Take any past participle of a transitive verb and write after this synopsis, and you have put the verb in the passive voice.

Now, if after the same synopsis we put the present participle of the verb, we shall have the progressive form of the verb, and not the passive voice; as, I am writing, they are writing, we shall be writing, etc.

Mistakes are often made when persons see parts of the verb to be, and conclude that the verb is in the passive voice; but the test is, does the subject act? For while active and passive are shown by the form of the verb, it is really the subject that is active or passive.

We have one other attribute to account for, namely **mood**, which means the **manner** of expressing our thought; as, the indicative, which declares a thing to be so; the potential, showing that a thing may be so; the subjunctive, noting a condition; the infinitive, which cannot be used as a verb at all, but expresses the thought in a general or indefinite way, and is therefore used as a neuter noun.

Verbs have three participles, present, as writing; past, as written; perfect, as having written. The same participles in the passive voice are, being written, written, having been written.

The child will observe that the middle participle —written—has the same form in both the active and passive voice, hence we can only tell which voice is meant by the context.

The past passive participle is very useful, being a shortened form, not carrying with it the sign of tense or voice; as, the book **written** by your brother was readily sold. Observe how frequently this form of participle is used by writers. For an illustration from Thanatopsis: "**Scourged** to his dungeon, but **sustained** and **soothed** by an unfaltering trust."

Shortened forms of expression are desirable, when they are not ambiguous. Many long-drawn-out sentences might be shortened and made more compact and forcible if the use of the participles were better known.

There are few points relating to tense and mood which the teacher will do well to call the pupils' attention to; as, **shall** in the first person denotes futurity, but in the second and third, determination; whereas, **will,** in the first person denotes determination, but in the second and third, futurity. To conjugate the future indicative correctly, we must say: I shall go, you will go, he will go. But if I say, I will go, you shall go, he shall go, it denotes determination.

Again, we must notice that the past tense refers to what is completely past; as, I saw your brother **yesterday.** We would not say, "I saw your brother today," as the time has not completely passed; I saw him yesterday, I have seen him today.

Again, we should not say, I intended to have written; but, I intended to write. I wanted to have seen the show, should be, I wanted to see the show. In each case the acts are present, with reference to the past time.

The old form of the subjunctive mood is passing out of use, and we are using the conditional indicative. Instead of saying, if he return by tomorrow, we say, if he returns.

The form of the present subjunctive is a contracted future; as, if he be innocent, means, if he shall be. Following the Latin construction, however, propositions which are impossible, or contrary to fact, should be expressed by the imperfect subjunctive; as, if I were you.

There are many other points in grammar which the teacher will find it necessary to explain to his pupils, if they would acquire the habit of correct speaking.

It is a good rule to remember that the distributive pronouns, each, every, either, neither, are always third person, singular number, and require the verb and pronoun to agree with them accordingly.

With reference to subject and predicate—and their modifiers—of sentences, they can be brought more clearly before us by a diagram than by an analysis with words.

Here is a little device for remembering the parts of speech:

A noun is the name of anything,
As school, or garden. hoop, or sv. ing.
Adjectives tell the kind of noun;
As great, small, pretty, white or brown.
Conjunctions join the words together;
As, bread and butter; wind or weather.
Verbs tell of something to be done;
As sing, or play or skip, or run.
A preposition stands before
A noun; as in or through a door
How things are done the adverbs tell;
As, slowly, quickly, ill or well.
An exclamation shows surprise;
As, ah! how pretty! oh! how wise!
Three little words you often see
Are articles; a or an and the.
Instead of nouns the pronoun stands;
Your book, his work, her hat, my hand.
The whole are called nine parts of speech;
Which reading, writing, speaking, teach.

This little bit of poetry saves us from many definitions, and it has helped many pupils who have understood it.

In arranging our sentences, we remember the kind of verbs we are using, as transitive verbs require an object to complete their meaning; as, the carpenters finished their work yesterday.

Carpenters finished work

| The | | yesterday | their |

The verbs that do not take an object are complete

in themselves.   Such are chiefly verbs of locomotion;
as, Mary has gone to her mother.

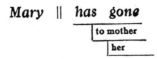

These are simple sentences, but when they are
compound or complex, or when the verb is in the im-
perative mood, they are not so easily diagramed; the
same is true when there are many modifiers both of
the subject and the predicate; and it is important to
know what clause a connective introduces; as, the day
seems gloomy, but the sun is shining behind the
clouds.

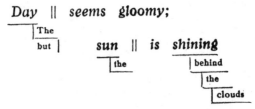

The man whom you sent did the work which was
required.

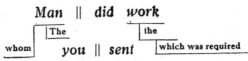

The pupil may remember that whatever answers
the question, when, where or how, is adverbial in
character; but, whatever answers the question, of what

kind, is adjective in character, especially **relative pronouns,** because they relate to some preceding noun, for a relative cannot represent an adjective.

The pupil will do well to notice how useful the word *that* is, for as a relative, it can relate to persons, lower animals and things; as, the man that you saw, and the cart that he rode in, brought back the dog that had run away.

It is also used as a connective, and as a demonstrative; as, I saw that that book would not answer the purpose; the first **that** being a connective, and the second a demonstrative.

We give children a great deal of poetry to learn; this involves the question of metre—or measure. To read poetry correctly, the right words must be accented.

In scanning a line of poetry, a measure consisting of one foot is called a monometre; two feet, a dimetre; three feet; a trimetre; four feet, a tetrametre; five feet, a pentametre; six feet, a hexametre, etc.

The iambus consists of a short and a long syllable, and this foot is principally the one used in English verse. To illustrate:

> "From all that dwell below the skies,
> Let the Creator's praise arise."

This is the long metre, and consists of all iambic tetrametres.

The common metre consists of tetrametres **and** trimetres alternating; as,

> "Jerusalem my happy home,
> Name ever dear to me."

The short metre is three iambic trimetres and one iambic tetrametre; as,

> Great is the Lord, our God,
> And let His praise be great;
> He makes His churches His abode,
> His most delightful seat.

The iambic pentametre is used in epic verse, and corresponds to the Latin hexametre; as,

> Stretch forth thy hand to God, 'tis not for thee
> To question aught, nor all His purpose see.
> The hand that led thee through the dreary night,
> Does not thy counsel need when comes the light.

The opposite of the iambus is the trochee. The dactyl—Greek for finger—has one long and two short syllables.

The opposite of the dactyl is the anapaest, two short and one long syllable.

A beautiful illustration of the trochaic metre is Longfellow's Psalm of Life:

> "Tell me not in mournful numbers,
> Life is but an empty dream;
> For the soul is dead that slumbers
> And things are not what they seem."

X.

HOW TO TEACH GEOGRAPHY

 THINK a great mistake is made by giving to those who begin geography a book to begin the study. As we are going to teach about this earth, its form, etc., why not begin with a ball? But as the child will find it difficult to conceive of a round object, let us make for him the continents of North and South America on a board, showing him where the mountains and rivers are found, and having him help us all that he can, putting the Rocky Mountains in their place and then the Sierras, and lastly the Coast Range, so called because they are so near the coast and accounting for the fact that the rivers are very short on that side. The teacher will need some strings of different lengths to show the Mississippi and Missouri Rivers, but all this must go on very slowly, for the child must learn what we mean by elevations and depressions. He must make the Great Lakes of North America and show their outlet, the St. Lawrence River, carrying their waters into the Atlantic Ocean. Rivers must run as the land slopes, and as the Mississippi flows south and the St. Lawrence flows in an easterly direction, it shows there must

be a high ridge of land between them, so that one river is turned south and the other in an easterly direction.

Little by little the child must learn the names of the bodies of water; why one is called a river, and all that he can tell you about a river. Names of bodies of land and water are very interesting to the child when he himself has made the picture of them on his map and can see the difference between a strait and an isthmus, the formation and use being the same, but one is water and the other is land; the difference between an island and a lake, one being land surrounded by water and the other being water surrounded by land. Little by little he goes over both continents, learning the names of the bodies of land and, of course, learning to spell them correctly. When we have thus prepared both continents, we lay off the bounds of the people who inhabit this land.

We suppose that the child has learned something about climate, why some parts are cold and some hot, and so, when he plants his people in the northern parts of the continents.

good time for him to be introduced to the Esquimaux, and, traveling farther south, he finds different people living in different parts, differing in their appearances or looks and in their occupations.

The study now becomes more interesting, as the child can fill out for himself the characteristics and the industries of the people who live in the different part, he knows that it is very cold there. Now is a

A very good picture of the globe can be made by a newspaper on which a line may be drawn showing the equator, then drawing another line a quarter of the way from the top, we may lay off the cold zone; and the torrid or hot zone, lying on both sides of the equator, can be equally well shown. Between the very hot and the very cold is the one which we call temperate, and now we can teach about the different seasons, the very hot and the very cold, having only two.

In the meantime, constant map drawing has prepared the pupil to draw upon the board that part of the country in which he lives, and another world of research and inquiry is open to him, and now he finds out facts for himself without having them forced upon him. When the pupils come into the geography room, there should be pictures of different lands, and as many specimens of the objects about them as they can get. Many questions in physical geography, that is, the geography of nature, will come up in the beginning lessons of geography, and are oftentimes very interesting; as, how does the water get into the clouds from the land; into the river; from the river into the sea; from the sea into the air; into the clouds; from the clouds upon the land again, and from the land into the river? Why the water of the Gulf of Mexico is warm? Some have said there are hot springs of water at its base.

The lightning and thunder form a fruitful subject to teach the children all about electricity, and

the man who discovered that lightning and electricity
are the same.

In teaching mathematical geography, the teacher
will need two circles which he can easily make out
of ordinary wire. The number of degrees in a circle,
the half of one, the quarter of one, can easily be
taught. That the earth is round cannot be demonstrated to very young people, but people have traveled
around it, starting from one point and coming back
to the same, and people have sailed around it. Now
the distance around all round bodies, is three hundred
and sixty degrees, and the half, one hundred and
eighty, and the quarter is ninety. We know that all
these lines upon the surface of the earth are merely
imaginary, and are placed on our globes for convenience. For instance, we take a line to reach around
the earth equally from the north and south poles, as
we call them; and we call this the equator.

We know that when the sun shines farthest north,
it will reach exactly twenty-three and a half degrees
over the north pole, and we put a circle there to mark
this distance, and call it the arctic circle. Now when
it begins to recede or go back, as it were, and reaches
the southernmost limit, it shines twenty-three and a
half degrees over the south pole, and we draw a
line, which, being opposite to the Arctic, we call the
Antarctic circle. Again, when the rays strike down
perpendicularly, we notice that they never go farther
than twenty-three and a half degrees north of our
middle line, and twenty-three and a half degrees south

of our middle line, or equator. We speak of the sun being overhead here at twelve o'clock, but the sun is never overhead out of the tropics. We call these limitation lines tropics, or turning points, because when the sun gets to one, it seems to turn back to the other. This limitation of the sun's vertical rays on the north is called the tropic of cancer, and the opposite one on the south is called the tropic of capricorn. Now, as cancer means a crab, and capricorn means a goat, why in the world should these circles be thus named? We shall have to answer this question by referring to the ancients' study of astronomy.

The heavens were a fruitful source of study to the ancients; and the groups of stars, which are constellations, received certain names, according to whatever they seemed to resemble. The group toward the north looked to them like a crab, and the one toward the south looked to them like a goat.

I found an old table, and drew a line upon it to represent the equator. I found some sand, and having drawn an outline of the eastern and western continents, I took the sand and made the elevations and depressions on both sides. The children could see where the tropic of cancer struck on the western continent, and trace it across to the eastern.

Keeping such an illustrative map before the eyes of the pupils, they can get a practical idea of the relative position and climate of places on both continents. Questions of latitude and longitude can best be settled in this way.

When we take from ninety degrees the limitation of the Arctic circle (twenty-three degrees on the south being the limit of the vertical rays of the sun) we have left forty-three degrees, the width of the north temperate zone, bounded on the north by the Arctic circle, and on the south by the Antarctic circle, and on the north by the Tropic of Capricorn. We find four seasons in the temperate zone, which we call Spring, Summer, Autumn and Winter; and the torrid zone, two, the wet and the dry; and in the frigid zone a very short summer and a long, cold winter. We have called the spaces thus marked off by rays of the sun zones, or belts, because they are parallel portions of the earth's surface. The Eastern Hemisphere is more difficult to mould and draw than the Western, and it is well to have them both on the other lines put in their places, and then the pupil can compare the climate on the Western Hemisphere. Having the zones marked off, they can easily tell us how many seasons each one of those countries has. I should like the children to know where the words arctic, cancer and capricorn come from. A constellation is a bunch of stars, or a number of stars taken together, which form a certain figure in the heavens. For instance, the children have all seen in the heavens, probably, what we call the big dipper, and the little dipper, because they look like dippers, having a bowl and a curved handle. Another name for these two constellations is Ursa Major and Ursa Minor; or, big bear and little bear.

A few lessons in astronomy upon the simplest

facts will open the door to interest the children, and
when they are able to study the great science of astronomy they can learn a great deal more. With two
circles made of wire, the teacher can represent the
equator.

Traveling on any round body is measured in degrees, minutes, seconds, etc. As the sun moves from
west to east, but seems to travel from east to west,
we can show that every fifteen degrees on the earth's
surface, going toward the east, bring us nearer the
sun by one hour of time, so we can go on and show
that when we have traveled seventy-five degrees toward the east, we will find the time at the end of our
journey to be five hours later than at the place we
started from. Therefore, as we travel toward the east,
which may be called the rising sun, we will find that
our time is faster than that which we left, and we can
keep on that way until we get half way around the
globe, and then we shall find that when it is ten
o'clock at night over on the other side of the globe it
is ten o'clock in the morning on this side. Many illustrations should be given about time to make it
plain to children about the movements of the sun,
and then they will understand what we mean by
standard time. The most delightful part of geography
is when we can begin teaching by journeys. Now to-
morrow we are going to make a visit to England, and
we will ask the children to find out how long it will
take us to get there; and whether we go by land or
sea; and what great city should we go to see when we

7

get there; how we should get across the great Atlantic Ocean; how many miles wide it is, what city we would start from on this side, and what line of steamships would we take and why; the different kind of sailing vessels.

And then the story of Columbus, and how he first came over will be in order. How long it took him, and how long it takes one of our vessels now. How much coal it takes to last one of these steamers across the ocean, and what is the average time for crossing. It will be seen that the teacher must be well furnished with information of a practical character. Keeping the moulded map of the two continents before the children's eyes, they can readily trace their way from one country to another, and tell where they could go by land, and how far they must go by water. How the people of different countries are employed is a very important subject, for we mean, how do they get their living; how do they find the means of sustenance?

Then comes the question, why are some nations employed in agriculture and why some are engaged in manufacturing, and some in mining, and some in trade and transportation; and what we mean by those engaged in commerce, foreign and domestic; and in this way we call attention to different occupations of the people who live on the earth. The difference in the clothing and food of people in the different countries will also claim our attention. And when we get ready to make these imaginary journeys, each child can be taught that it must pack its trunk with the kind of

clothes it will probably need, and this will make a
great deal of merriment. This is caused by the children not understanding about climate, the difference
in the towns on the sea coast, and the towns in the interior. This also calls up the question where all the
great cities on the globe are located, and why. The
history of the people on the globe is a most interesting
one. Where did the people of our own country, the
Western settlers, come from; and why did they come?
Little by little the children learn much about our country from their geographical travels, and the story of
Columbus is like a fairy tale. How he set out westward to find a northwest passage to India. For he
believed that the earth was round and he knew nothing
of the great continent lying between. So starting out,
he was three months with his three little ships sailing
about on the ocean, and when he came to the American
continents he supposed he had come to India, and for
that reason he called the first land he came to, the West
Indies, and the island, he called Hispaniola, or Little
Spain. It was not until Amerigo discovered the main-
land that it was known that not an island, but a whole
new world had been discovered by Columbus. The
history of this great man is full of romance, and the
teacher has a fine field to get the children to thinking
and to draw out their thoughts when this subject
comes up. Why had sailors always gone eastward
when they wanted to go to India? Why had they
never ventured beyond what is called the pillars of
Hercules, that is, beyond the strait of Gibraltar, lead-

ing out into the Atlantic Ocean? An old writer has
said: For years and years mankind had confined himself to the Mediterranean Sea, and there we lived like
frogs in a pond.

The history of the compass must now be studied,
for by its invention mankind was no longer confined to
any one place of the earth's surface, but the needle,
always pointing to the north, became a sure guide
when they were looking for a strange place; and so
Columbus could tell in what direction he was sailing,
because then men knew the use of the compass. The
question may arise, why does the needle point to the
north? It is because of the magnetic attraction of the
north pole. The compass is divided into thirty-two
parts, and when a sailor knows all of these points he
is said to be able to box the compass.

Little by little, discovery has traced the lightning
to its source. Benjamin Franklin found this out, and
as soon as men knew what it was, they made machines
and harnessed its powerful force into their service,
and made it to carry their messages over the whole
world, and by it we talk to people hundreds of miles
away; aye, thousands of miles away. And when men
stop wrangling and hating one another, they will
begin to learn more of scientific law, and we may have
wireless telephone, not only extending over this earth,
but extending to the moon and to Mars.

We are now trembling on the eve of a great discovery which I have said God will show us when we
delight to know more of His way. At first it was

thought we could only talk by the telephone a few miles apart, but now we have the long distance telephone. Who would have ever believed that cables could be laid in the deep ocean to carry the telegraphic message. But by wireless telegraphy the cable may now be displaced, and it is not too much to suppose that it will not be many years before we shall be able to talk with the people on Mars, and if there are none in the moon we shall be able to know it! but we can easily imagine that all the great planets swinging in space are not there for nothing. When we use the Orrery, we see the position of this earth among the other heavenly bodies, and we see that it is so small and insignificant in size that it looks like a mere ball of putty, and yet we allow our thoughts and aspirations to be limited by its twenty-five thousand miles of circumference.

Unholy ambition never succeeds well in anything, nor will the Great Creator of the universe reveal His secrets to those whose only desire is to shine in the eyes of men. But the light of Heaven will shine all around the man who humbly and fervently asks for more light, more light.

XI

POINTS IN ARITHMETIC

No. 1—Beginning Arithmetic
  1. Making and writing numbers.

No. 2—Making and learning the Multiplication table
  1. Reason for it

No. 3—Simple Application
  1. Counting by 5's, counting by 10's.
  2. Finding cost of simple articles.
  3. Making change by running up to a naught or five.
  4. Keeping store.

No. 4—Investigating the Multiplication table
  1. Finding square and cube.
  2. Naming and defining.
  3. Evolution and involution.
  4. Powers and roots.
  5. Having a fractional part of a number to find it.
  6. So many times a number to find it.
  7. Complete divisors.
  8. Divisors with remainders over.

No. 5—Preparation for long division by divisions of the multiplication table

No. 6—Illustrating axioms
  1. Square of the sum of two numbers.
  2. Square of the difference of two numbers.
  3. The rectangle of the sum and difference.

No. 7—The L. C. M. and G. C. D.
  1. Principles. Underline them.

No. 8—Reduction of Common fractions
   1. How to add, subtract, multiply and divide them.

No. 9—Show that the same principles apply to decimals and reasons for pointing in decimals

No. 10—Interest

No. 11—Finding what part one number is of another

No. 12—Ratio and Proportion

No. 13—Compound numbers

No. 14—Mensuration

No. 15—Arithmetical and Geometrical progression

There are only two things we can do in arithmetic, put together and take apart. **Multiplication** is a quick way to **add** and **Division** is a quick way to **subtract**. Show these two processes by several examples.

It has often been asked, how shall I begin numbers? We begin by counting and making the numbers up to ten. Be careful, in making numbers, to make them neatly. Do not make a 4 like an x nor a 7 like a 9; nor make a 5 with the stem flying in the air. The children can count, for practice, any article in the room. Begin as soon as possible the **Multiplication table,** for that is one of the best instruments that I know of in teaching arithmetic. Problems may easily be learned in **simple multiplication** which we would suppose to belong to higher arithmetic. I do not see why we should not go from 1 to 25, although it is usual to stop at 12. Teaching the **squares** and **cubes** found in them is very helpful, and assists in solving many apparently difficult problems.

Counting by 5's and counting by 10's backward and forward. Making change by running up to a naught or a five. Finding cost of simple articles in a grocery.

We find that Foreigners seldom make a mistake in handling our money in the markets and stores. Illustration: You buy something that comes to 33 cents; 33 and 2, 35; and 5, 40; and 10, 50; and you gave 50 cts., and you know you have your right change. 10, 5, 2 equals 17. The other, and less convenient way, would be to put down 33 under 50 and subtract.

Define powers and roots. Let us see what powers we can get out of the tables 3's, 4's, 5's, etc. Whenever we **multiply** a number into itself we get a power, as: 5^5s, 3^3s, 8^8s, 7^7s. **Roots of numbers** are those **equal factors,** which **multiplied** together will produce them. Cube root, one of the 3 equal factors, square root one of the 2 equal factors, as: square root of 64 is 8. Cube root of 64 is 4.

In finding the cost of simple articles in play store, etc., we found it necessary to give good attention to dates.

How many threes can you get out of 21, how many out of 24, 36? How many fives can you get out of 15, how many out of 20, how many out of 40? Then divisors with remainders over, as: How many fives can you get out of 17, how many out of 29, and what over? As, I bought 4 lbs. of sugar at 5 cts. a pound. How much change have I from a quarter? I bought

5 lbs. of sugar at 5½ cts. lb. How much change ought
I to have from 25 cts.?

So many times a number to find it. **Fractional part**
of a number to find it, as: 12 is 4 times what number?
3 times, 6 times, 12 times. These same questions
must be asked with other multiples. 8 is ⅓ of what
number? ¼, ⅕, etc. Now put the two together and
ask, 12 is ⅜ of what number? ⅘ of what number?

I have shown how much can be taught by using
the multiplication table as an instrument and how it
will lead out in higher arithmetic. After reading and
writing numbers up to ten, go on to a hundred.

And now we must teach the difference in value
according to place. To show that the first period is
ones, second is thousands, third is millions.
<u>100</u>, <u>100</u>, <u>100</u>.

Show how these differ according to the period
they are in. Write a hundred in each one. The first
is 100 ones, the second is 100 thousand, the third, 100
millions.

In order to read a number correctly, separate it
into periods of three figures each, beginning at the
right. Remember that the first period is ones, second
thousands, third millions, fourth billions, fifth trillions,
and so on.

Extension means the act of drawing out; extension in one direction gives a line; extension in two
directions gives a surface; extension in three directions
gives a solid. So we notice that linear measure is the
measure of lines. A surface has two dimensions, length

and breadth. So we measure surface by square measure.

A solid has three dimensions, length, breadth and thickness; so we measure solids by cubic measure.

Capacity means extent of room or space. There are two measures of capacity, liquid and dry measures.

The distance around an angular object is called **perimeter.** The distance around a round object is called **circumference.** In order to find the perimeter of a rectangle, add the length to the breadth and multiply by two. When you add the length and breadth together, we get half way around, and so we multiply by two to get the whole distance.

In order to get the area of a rectangle, multiply the length by breadth; as, give to each unit in length one unit in breadth, and we shall then have 12 square units; there will be as many rows of these as there are units in the breadth. If one row contains 8 units, twelve rows contain 12 x 8 units, or 96 units. If we should multiply the length by the breadth, we should have the same result. To find the number of cubic inches, multiply length, breadth and height together. One of the best ways to get work quickly given out is to have it written down on manila paper.

First, the board is clean; second, one division is sent to the board; third, while they are facing the teacher, some pupil passes the papers around. There must be no time for picking or choosing. Then each one turns to the board and begins to work. The teacher must keep his class doing regular work in reviewing exercises. One half of the work should be reviewed every day. When children first begin to think about a subject they cannot possibly take in all at once; here is where teachers often make mistakes. When a child is learning a rule, he has only begun. He will learn more little by little. Every time the review is given the children learn something new about the subject. There should be frequent mental exercise. A teacher must think more comprehensively than his pupil.

Reading signs is very important, especially for pupils who are beginning, as:

$8 + 4, 8 - 4, 8 \div 4$, or $10 - 5, 10 \div 5, 10 + 5$. Letting the child see the different operations.

How can a teacher teach mental arithmetic and practical arithmetic at the same time? About forty-five minutes is given to a class in arithmetic, and if we should add to this fifteen minutes to mental drill, it would give more time to arithmetic than its share, considering the other studies.

But if the teacher separates the class in two divisions, then one set can be doing practical work while the other is getting mental drill.

The mental drill is exceedingly important.

The teacher can do a great deal in ten minutes and give a variety of exercises very useful in building up mental power.

The second division of the class can be doing practical work at the board or while seated.

There should be two ways in examining a class

in arithmetic. First—one is to see if the pupil can handle large numbers and is accurate in his work, and then we must not give more than four or five examples.

Second—We must examine in power of reasoning; then we can give ten problems with numbers of two places, as: Find the sum of ½ of 20; ⅓ of 18; ⅙ of 40 cts.

John earns one day ½ of a dollar, another day ⅒ of $1.00; he afterward spent ¼ of $1.00.

If rice is 9 cts. a lb., how many lbs. can you get for 96 cts.?

John has 20 cts., and this is ⅔ of Mary's money; how much has Mary? And many such simple examples should be given, which will show you how much your pupil can reason.

From the sum of 20 and 30 take their difference.

Multiply the sum of 8 + 6 by their difference and add 4 to the result. Divide the sum of 4 and 16 by ⅓ of their difference.

From the product of five times 8 take three times 2 and add 50 to the result.

To the quotient 27 divided by 3 add their product plus their sum.

$$25 \div 5416 \times 2 - 6 \div 2 = ?$$
$$25 - 5 \times 5 + 10 - 2 \times 5 = ?$$

It is never necessary to wait and do nothing, but while we are waiting we can always find something else to do, and so make good use of the time. Remember Washington Irving, who became a learned man by

using his spare minutes for reading. And remember
Elihu Burritt; he is called the learned blacksmith.
During his spare moments he learned fifty languages.
Let us learn what to do with odds and ends of time.
When the sum and difference of two numbers is given,
to find the numbers, add the difference to the sum,
and we get twice the greater number. When we have
twice the number and divide by two, we get the
number.

One fractional part of a number is one fractional
part of another number. Several fractional parts of
numbers are several fractional parts of another number,
as: $\frac{1}{4}$ of 20 is $\frac{1}{7}$ of what number; $\frac{3}{4}$ of 20 is $\frac{5}{9}$ of
what number?

Beginning children in numbers is harder than any
other part of the work. First, they must be taught to
count consecutively up to one hundred, and at the
same time the counting must be done with objects:
rose leaves, grains of corn or the objects in the room.

Addition, multiplication, division made all at once:
No good teacher will think of following the book.
Take any number of objects, say 10, with a board in
front; objects laid out in piles of ten. Take one away,
count the number left, then $9 + 1 = 10$, until the child
understands. Take 3, 5 away, see what is left. Then
separate ten in five equal parts, some one making piles
of two, and see how many piles are in 10. The child
sees five piles with two each equal 10, or, $5 \times 2 = 10$.
After this, abstract reasoning immediately; show use
of it. As, bread is 5 cts. a loaf, how many can we get

for 10 cts.? One yeast cake at 2 cts. and one loaf of bread from 10, how many have you left? And many problems of like character.

The teacher who is a master of the multiplication table will find he has a means of investigation in arithmetic and algebra all ready to his hand. The factors which produce certain products, the squares and cubes hidden away in their depths, all come to light before they are hidden away in some apparently difficult problem in proportion or percentage.

The teacher who is expert in the use of multiplication table can easily teach involution and evolution, proportion and other apparently difficult processes in arithmetic and algebra in this simple way. Now is the time to teach the square of the sum, the square of the difference and the rectangle of the sum and difference, thus preparing for algebra. It is well just here to define what we mean by the numerical square and the geometrical square. The numerical square being the product of the two equal factors, and the geometrical square an equilateral rectangle; also the numerical cube being the product of three equal factors, and the geometrical cube a solid bounded by six equal squares.

The teacher must go into his room, having prepared the work in arithmetic and algebra as far as the learners have advanced. Do not be satisfied with the few problems which their books upon the subject present. The teacher should have consulted ten or twenty books on the same subject and come to his class prepared to test the children's knowledge upon what they are learning, and their ability to understand the principles and to handle the work with success.

Our knowledge in mathematics is largely increased by what we know of the right-angle triangle and of the ratio between numbers, and I have said this can be taught when we are studying the multiplication table, as: 5 : 7 :: 15 : some number. Now it is common in proportion to say, when three terms are given, multiply the means together and divide by the other extreme, or multiply the extremes together and divide by the given means. Now 5 is the same part of 7 that 15 is of some number. We know that 5 is $\frac{5}{7}$ of 7, so 15 must be $\frac{5}{7}$ of some number. If 15 is $\frac{5}{7}$, $\frac{1}{7}$ must be $\frac{1}{5}$ of 15, or 3. And $\frac{7}{7}$, or the whole, will be 7 × 3, or 21; therefore 5 : 7 :: 15 : 21. So we see the great importance of teaching what part one number is of another as leading out afterwards to ratio and proportion.

A good rule for long division: Try the first figures of the divisor into the first figures of the dividend, and about as many times as it is contained, about so many times the whole divisor will be contained into the whole dividend. You may have heard of the poet who made a coop for his chickens. He made a big door for the big chickens and a little door for the little chickens. Now, which door was not necessary?

Numbers in English are written upon a geometrical progression of ten, and a number standing in front of a number is ten times greater than the number back of it and a hundred times greater than the one back of that, and a thousand times greater than the first one, and standing in the fifth place, ten thousand times greater. This rapid increase soon places the head numbers out of sight of the back ones. That is the reason we call the head numbers the big chickens. We call the first figures of the divisor the big chickens and the corresponding one of the dividend the big door. In long division, if you have a remainder greater than the divisor, then the figure in the quotient is too small. A very useful rule in mathematics is to always prove your subtraction. Instead of using the terms subtrahend and minuend, etc., say, add what you take away to what you had left, and if you get what you had at first the work is right. It will be some time before they completely realize what you take away is the subtrahend, and what you have left the remainder, and minuend the sum to be diminished.

To add, subtract, multiply and divide fractions need not be at all difficult. We mean by reducing to a common denominator, making the parts equal in size. We can then see how many we have, find the difference between them or see how many times one is contained into another. When we are reducing to a common denominator we are multiplying fractions, as: We have one apple divided into 3 parts and another divided into 2 parts; we will take one of the 3 equal parts, which is ⅓, and one of the 2 equal parts, which is $\frac{1}{2}$. We will cut each third into 2 equal parts, thus getting $\frac{1}{2}$ of $\frac{1}{3}$ and we see that the whole unit consists of six of those parts; so $\frac{1}{2}$ of $\frac{1}{3}$ is $\frac{1}{6}$. Then we cut each half in three equal parts; the unit will consist of 6 of those parts, and we see that $\frac{1}{3}$ of $\frac{1}{2} = \frac{1}{6}$ of a whole. Now if we had $\frac{1}{3}$ and $\frac{1}{2}$ of anything we can see that it is $\frac{5}{6}$ of the whole.

We also see that $\frac{3}{6} - \frac{2}{6} = \frac{1}{6}$. Again $\frac{1}{2} \div \frac{1}{3} = \frac{3}{6} \div \frac{2}{6} = 1\frac{1}{2}$. The question is how much of the greater can you measure off on the smaller; 3 cannot be measured off on 2, but we can measure off $\frac{2}{3}$ of the measuring line—$\frac{1}{3} \div \frac{1}{2} = \frac{2}{3}$. The same principles apply to **decimal fractions.** These are very beautiful and very important, because we use them in finding interest.

It can easily be shown that it is not difficult to tell what rate of interest is being received on any sum of money, and it is now very important that we should teach interest in a businesslike way, and remember that percentage is not interest. First find the cost of what we bought, and to this sum add all the after expenses, then see what rate per cent. this is on our money.

As a general thing, bookkeeping is left for the higher classes, but it ought to be taught much lower down, and it is for this reason that decimals, which can be so easily used in the operation of finding interest, should be well taught. For instance: A house is bought for $3000 and rents for $25 a month; what rate of interest does the investment pay? Nothing was said of taxes, nothing of the repairs and nothing of the

8

time when the house was unrented, and yet this was given as a problem for some one to find the rate of interest. A good rule is to find what the money would have gained if it had been on interest at one per cent. for the given time and divide the given interest by it.

XII

MY VISIT TO ENGLAND.

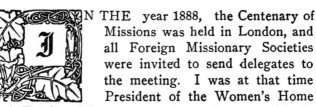N THE year 1888, the Centenary of Missions was held in London, and all Foreign Missionary Societies were invited to send delegates to the meeting. I was at that time President of the Women's Home and Foreign Missionary Society of the A. M. E. Church, and was elected a delegate to represent the Society at that meeting. For the better understanding of the work, I went to New York and met the different heads of the Societies in America. Among these was Doctor Kincaid, a classmate of mine at Oberlin College, and a representative minister in his church.

Doctor Kincaid reminded me of an incident which happened at Oberlin, when he and I, among others, were examined for the First Church choir. He asked if I remembered how sorry I was when he failed in his examination. I certainly had forgotten all about it.

When the time came for me to go to England, I did not look upon the visit with much favor. Never having been abroad before, and not knowing a soul on the ship, I had many doubts as to how I would get

along. And so I had it out with the Lord. Thou seest,
O Lord, that I have no one to help me, and if I get
nausea I may faint and be very troublesome to those
about me. Thou seest, O Lord, that I must not get
sick. And I wasn't sick.

From time to time, when I had the least feeling of
nausea, I would walk up and down the deck of the
vessel and sing. Patriotic songs, Sunday school
hymns, all came in for a share of my singing devotion.

It so happened that the French Minister to Mada-
gascar was aboard the ship; and as the notes of that
noble melody, the Marseillaise, rolled out upon the water,
he expressed himself as being delighted, and what
Frenchman wouldn't. So, I began to make friends.
Not less, also, when the "Star Spangled Banner" came
up for a share. I knew that I could sing as much as I
pleased; nobody was disturbed, and the least inkling of
sickness entirely disappeared. I can recommend singing as one of the best preventatives against sea-
sickness.

We arrived at Liverpool. Out in the Mersey the
ship was blowing and blowing. I asked what this
was for, and was told that it was a call for a tender.
What is that? said I. Very soon I saw a little steamer
leaving the wharf and coming toward us, bobbing up
and down like a duck.

Soon we were at the Custom House where the
officers were waiting to examine our "luggage," as
they call it there. It didn't take long to get thru
mine, but a dear old Irish friend that I had made on

the vessel got held up on some little bags of candy which she was taking to her grandchildren. It's tobacco, said the officer. It's candy, said my Irish friend. I felt that I could not remain longer, for the cab was waiting to take us to the train. But my friend came out with the verdict in favor of candy.

Having arrived at the train, my friend said, I am going to cable home. One word tells the story. What is your code? I had no code. Did not understand what a convenience it was. One word could have informed friends at home that I arrived safe and in good condition. My Irish friend had often crossed the water and had learned what to do. I should have decided upon a code before I left home. As it was, they had to wait at home until they could hear from me by letter.

Off for London now, where Edwards' Family Hotel gave me safe shelter until I could communicate with the committee.

This having been attended to at Exeter Hall, I was informed that Lady ——— had signified her intention to take some of the delegates. I thought it no more than fair that she should be informed that I was a colored woman. Ah shucks, said the committee, we do not care anything about that.

And so off I went to what turned out to be a most agreeable stopping place.

Next came the meeting with that assembly of gray-headed men and women, who for many years had been living in far-away lands, carrying the Gospel into the benighted places of the earth.

What a glorious thing it was to hear their experiences. Fairy stories could not be more entrancing.

I knew that there was much to be seen in London, but I could not be lured away from this religious assembly, so long as the meetings continued.

In a few days I was informed that Dr. William B. Derrick had arrived from America and was eloquently giving his story of the uplift among his people.

The English people were deeply touched by the fact that, tho hardly a decade out of slavery, the colored people had organized for work in heathen lands.

A Presbyterian minister, in speaking, told the women repeatedly that they must not assume any ecclesiastical functions. This got me riled, and in reply I tried to make it plain that the Lord God alone gives the limit to the functions of woman's religious work. I never had any desire to assume ecclesiastical functions, and I always considered the pulpit a sacred place, and therefore have always refused to make speeches from it.

In addressing the meeting, I spoke in part as follows, (taken from the printed minutes): Sometimes when a thought comes uppermost it is better to get it out of the way, as it may be very troublesome afterwards. Now, with reference to what we have heard this morning, I wish to say this. I think there is nothing in the law of God's universe, that was made without having ample space to move in, without trenching upon its neighbor's domain; and it may very well be said of women, that while they are and were created second, they were not only created with body, but they were created also with a head, and they are responsible therefore to decide in certain matters and to use their own judgment.

It is also very true, as I will certainly say, that fools often rush in where angels fear to tread; but then I question as to whether all fools are confined to the feminine gender. Ladies and gentlemen, time is very brief, indeed, and I am overwhelmed with the thoughts of looking upon English people and upon English faces, the historic land of liberty. No one here can understand how the women occupying the great seaboard yonder, have looked upon this land— those who, like myself, bear the yoke with them. Now, there are in the United States, distributed among eleven of the former Southern States, over eight million of my people. Of these, more than 3,000,000 are women, and those three millions whom the Lord God, in His inscrutable providence, has seen fit to pass through a hard school, distributed, as I say, along there and very nearly in the majority, they send greetings here today and wish me to speak about what their feeling is towards the Christianization of the colored races of the earth. You will not, I am sure, deny us the very peculiar interest, as I say, in the Christianization of all races. These poor women, less than a decade out of slavery, established a Foreign Missionary Society and have their foreign missionaries in the island of

Hayti, in San Domingo, in Trinidad, in St. Thomas and Sierra Leone, on the west coast of Africa. They have not a whole loaf to share, as we all know; they have not even a half loaf to share with their sisters and brothers in foreign lands. They have but a crust; but, poor as they are, they sent me here—three millions of those women sent me 3000 miles—to say to all who are here assembled that their hearts are in that work, and that they intend to devote not only what little they have of money and resources to sustain their missionaries in those lands, but they are prepared to give themselves.

How I wanted yesterday to say, as Mr. Guinness spoke of Africa, what wonderful transmutations under God's providence have been taking place among these people, and what a missionary spirit has been developed amongst them. The problem how to reach the colored people on the Western Coast has been for years one which civilized nations have been unable to unravel, but He, in His own time, will make it plain. Who hath known the mind of the Lord in those things? And yet we have been hampered on all sides by presupposed ideas of what was meant by the enslavement of all these people. Now, let me say something about them. The spirit of missionaries, the spirit of mission work, is the spirit of sharing all we have. Those to whom God gives intelligence and wealth, He gave it simply that it might be shared. Did He give you more intelligence than another? Then He gave some one else less, and it is your bounden duty to use it to help that one who has not so much as you. Did He make you rich? Then He has made another poor, and the greatest of blessings, and the truest happiness is to share all that you have with those who need it. But if not from the grace and blessedness, I do think from the very necessity of the fact that all history teaches that those who have had more light from God, or more of the good things of this life, and who have not shared it with those about them, they have had every bit taken away from them, as you very well know ; and the light passed on, and on, and on, thru the Eastern countries, westward until it beamed equally on all men, as the Lord God intended that it should do.

XIII.

MY VISIT TO SOUTH AFRICA..

O GO to Africa, the original home of our people, see them in their native life and habits, and to contribute, even in a small degree, toward the development, civil and religious, that is going on among them, is a privilege that anyone might be glad to enjoy.

After having spent thirty-seven years in the school room, laboring to give a correct start in life to the youth that came under my influence, it was indeed, to me, a fortunate incident to finish my active work right in Africa, the home of the ancestors of those whose lives I had endeavored to direct.

All this came about thru my marriage in 1881 to Rev. L. J. Coppin who, in 1900, was elected one of the Bishops of the African Methodist Episcopal Church, and assigned to South Africa.

It may not be of special interest to the reader to hear all about the trip across the Atlantic to Liverpool on the steamship Umbria, of the Cunard Line, nor of the voyage from London, down the river Thames to Southampton, on the steamship German, and thence down the coast via Teneriffe Island.

The objective point was Cape Town, South Africa, and when on Sunday morning, November 30, 1902, we came to anchor in Table Bay, a new world seemed to rise before me, and a new vision.

Our new residence was at Cape Town, where rooms had been prepared on the second floor of a building, which constituted our headquarters when not traveling over the work.

Cape Town is, in a sense, a modern city. It has been occupied a long time by the English, and such sanitary conditions obtain as might be expected of a city under English rule.

The historic Table Mountain affords a natural reservoir, and supplies the town with drinking water of a superior quality. The markets are not large, and much of the food is imported, and the "high cost of living" is a familiar topic. Being situated right on the Bay, fishing is one of the daily vocations, and we have fish in abundance. But then, even missionaries will tire of fish if they are the daily food, for surely man can no more live on fish alone than on bread alone.

We were made as comfortable in our quarters as missionaries have reason to expect, and the one absorbing thought was, how shall we accomplish the work for which we left our homes.

In uniting with the A. M. E. Church after my marriage, I asked my husband what particular work I would be required or expected to do, and was told that a certain portion of missionary work was given by the Church to its women. Now, here was the field, for, with all the outward show of civilization at this English seaport, the needs of the native and "coloured" people were everywhere plain to be seen.

The colored people are the mixed bloods, a condition that obtains wherever a stronger people force their way into a country and take possession.

In many cases, the children of the dominant race were cared for by being given, at least, a primary education, and such employment as enabled them to have a fair proportion of the necessities of life. But the much larger portion of "Cape coloured" people were left to live their lives as best they might, and rear their children in or out of wedlock.

It was not an unusual sight to see my husband marry couples and at the same time baptise both their children and their grandchildren, and that within a very short distance of Cape Town.

The homes in which many of them lived in those nearby places might well be called huts, and very poor ones at that.

The Dutch farmers who gave them employment were largely engaged in grape farming, and the manufacture of wine, the poorest brands of which would be given to those miserable dependents as part wages.

In Cape Town itself, saloons were plentiful. Sometimes one on every corner of street after street, and occasionally one between.

It surely cannot be difficult to imagine how easily a people so neglected in the higher ideals of life would turn to the drink habit as a mere pastime.

The native people—those of unmixed African blood—who came down from the country beyond, and found employment principally as loaders and unloaders of ships, and the heavier work along the railroads, would be quartered in "Locations" a mile or two beyond the city limits. The cabins, or huts, provided for them by the government at Cape Town, are very inferior for comfort to those built by the natives in their rural habitat before being brought into contact with our so-called civilization. The Cape Town Location was on a tract of land that would be fairly flooded with water during the rainy season, and many who came down hale and hearty would return consumptives—a disease practically unknown to the "heathen" —or never return at all.

The drink habit would soon be learned by those raw natives, and their last state would become worse than the first.

We were often asked why we made our headquarters at Cape Town instead of going and remaining far away into the interior, doing work entirely among the uncivilized. But it was hard indeed for us to turn away entirely from the conditons that met us upon the very entrance into the country. It is true the bulk of our work was far away from Cape Town, and among people in primitive life; but it was a good thing to have a base at this seaport town, where occasionally we could ourselves return to modern life, and where we could also work among those who needed us quite as much as those who had not been introduced into the

blessedness (?) of a civilization that places the acquisition of wealth far above the redemption of souls.

Well, here my "special" work began. My husband, who preceded me on the field, had purchased a
building and turned it into a school and mission house
—Bethel Institute—and here I called the women together, the women who had risen above their environ-
ments, really noble, faithful, Christian women, and began my temperance work.

We organized after the model of our work at
home. A local society was started, not only at Cape
Town, but at many nearby places where we had mis-
sion stations, and, drawing from their membership, a
Conference Branch was organized for the Cape Colony
Conference.

At our first Annual Session of the Conference,
which met at Port Elizabeth, the sight of native and
colored women in a missionary session was one of the
features of the Conference; and a glorious and inspiring sight it was. Gathered about me on the platform,
and around the altar, were women who never before
had appeared in public for Christian work, at least,
never before to take a leading part in it. They had
been lately organized, and now they were called upon
to do the work of officers, and to speak to the public
gathering for themselves; some in Dutch—their
mother tongue—some in broken English, and some in
their own God-given native language.

In my travels over the work with my husband
I went as far as Bulawayo, 1360 miles from Cape

Town. The journey was long, tiresome and trying. At the meeting held there in our mission house, I had a new and not pleasant experience, for, after endeavoring to forget the fatigue caused by the journey, I made my accustomed address by the aid of an interpreter, and was seized with a fainting spell. I had for years been accustomed to hard work, and often deprivations, but had never before fallen at my post.

I was tenderly carried by the loving hands of native women out into the open, while Mr. Coppin went on with the meeting.

The small child of one of the native women was much disturbed when the mother left it in the care of others while she waited on me. The little one was not yet old enough to take in the situation, and so, openly revolted against such neglect, caused by a stranger who had been speaking in an unknown tongue.

At this particular meeting we afterwards learned that the government had spies on hand, native spies, to observe all that was said, and report to the authorities. The fear seemed to be that the instruction likely to be given to the natives would cause them to become dissatisfied with their lot, and, as some said, "bring on a native problem, as they had had a Boer problem." The spirit of suspicion was everywhere prevalent, and did much, for a time, to retard our work. I think, however, the authorities finally came to understand that we were missionaries pure and simple, and not politicians, and if there was any cause for alarm it must

grow out of the fact that enlightenment does indeed
enable people to see their true condition, and that they
do sometimes become dissatisfied when convinced that
injustice, and a general lack of the Christian spirit of
brotherhood, is responsible for much of their misery.

The route to Bulawayo is upon the road constructed by that great empire builder, John Cecil Rhodes,
with the view of carrying out his scheme, "from Cape
to Cairo." It goes thru a large portion of country
that is governed entirely by native chiefs, with, of
course, the English oversight that is now given to all
of South Africa, for there is no portion of the country
that is absolutely in the hands of native rulers, such
as obtained previous to the coming of the white man.
But, in those native colonies like Basutoland, for instance, the land is occupied by the people of a given
tribe, or "nation," as they like to call themselves, with
a chief—paramount chief—in authority. The chief is
the ruler and judge in all matters, not including capital
punishment, or the leasing of lands to foreigners. They
live their shepherd life and pay but little attention to
agriculture. Having learned the value of money as
an exchange, they go to the mining camps and work
for periods of time, six months, a year, or even more,
according to contract; take their money, return home,
buy cattle, and, if they wish, add more wives to their
household.

Many of them have never been away from their
desert homes, and when the trains pass periodically
thru their country, they come out to the Halts, where

water is taken on and telegraphic connections made. Those Halts, or stations, are in the care of English officials. Perhaps a man, his wife and their children are the only occupants of that home, away out into the desert, far removed from civilization, in the midst of native people, called heathen, who are counted by multiplied thousands, but they have no fear and suffer no harm.

These innocent children of the forest come out to meet the trains. They come in great numbers and in native garb, which cannot be called clothing, but merely a sheep skin, or strings of beads about their loins. They seem amazed as they gaze at the trains, filled with people so unlike themselves in appearance. They chatter away among themselves. Just what they are thinking and saying, their distinguished guests have no means of knowing.

But when we, as missionaries, turn aside and go among them with our interpreters, we have an opportunity to come in possession of their thoughts and find out what manner of people they are.

That which always seems to be the prevailing desire among them is to acquire a knowledge of the new conditions which they see, but cannot understand.

They soon learn what is meant by school, and immediately express a desire to have their children taught. In my experience among them, I have never found them entirely satisfied with mere abstract teaching of religion. They have religious views before we reach them. Crude, of course; unenlightened, uncer-

9

tain, speculative, false, just as all people hold who have not been given the true word of God. When those who come to them win their confidence, they readily modify their religious views, regarding their teachers as their superiors in matters religious. But there is nothing like a superstitious worshipping of their benefactors, nor of the new doctrines which they bring. With an incredible clearness of vision, they look forward to and expect some practical and really tangible benefits to grow out of their new relation.

They already have, as it were, an intuitive sense of right and wrong, hence they do no harm to the stranger in their midst. Indeed, our religious teaching is, in a sense, but an explanation of their own religious impulses.

In their own moral and religious ethics they teach thou shalt, and thou shalt not, without being able to give philosophical reasons for it. Now when light is thrown into their benighted minds, and reasons are given for certain ways of life required of them, and their own creeds revised, taken from and added to, imagine their surprise when they see their teachers, disregarding in their lives, their own teaching. With child-like credulity they turn from the old to the new, and when disappointed in those who bring them the light they are not prepared at first to conclude, by a process of reasoning, that there is chaff among the wheat, dross with the gold, but, rather, they feel that they have been deceived, and this accounts for some of the lapses of which we hear so much.

Our interpreters are native men who have come in contact with civilization by being trained at mission schools. Some of them have been to England and America and studied. But many of them have never been out of Africa, and yet they speak fluently English, Dutch and several of the tribal languages, and read the Bible in those languages. We are dependent upon the interpreter, and greatly indebted to the forerunners in the mission fields who made such indispensible aid possible.

On our way from Bulawayo we stopped at Mafeking and spent some time. There was a public reception given to us at the Masonic temple. Mafeking became famous during the Anglo-Boer war on account of the siege, and the gallant defense by General Baden-Powell.

John Cecil Rhodes was there during the siege, and when they brought him butter he refused to eat it, and sent it to the sick soldiers. Some of our societies were called the Cecil Rhodes Bands of Mercy.

Living at Mafeking are a large number of Malay people who are Mohammedans. The leading spirit among them is a merchant, Hadje Ben Hassen. Ben Hassen is his name, and he is a Hadje by virtue of having made a pilgrimage to Mecca. One of the moving spirits in the reception which was tendered was this Hadje. He headed a delegation of his countrymen and fellow religionists to the hall, and himself occupied a seat on the platform among the speakers. In his address he said that it was not customary for

Christians and Mohammedans to thus come together, but, as there was a Negro Bishop in their midst, he felt that the religious idea should be set aside, and that all should come out to do honor to a distinguished member of the race.

Some of the Mohammedan people sent their children to our school at Cape Town, and even provided them with Bibles that they might take part in the opening services of the school.

Perhaps one of the things that has caused Mohammedans to step over the religious barriers that have kept the dark races apart in Africa, is the fact that, when the lines of proscription are drawn—and this is becoming more and more so—the Malay, the Indian—East Indian—the native and the "coloured" are all treated alike in matters social. Some of the Malays and Indians are very wealthy, and the renewal of license has been refused to some of the Indian merchants because it was said that English merchants could not compete with them. This happened at Port Elizabeth during the time that we were there in conference sessions.

Much wisdom and patience will be required on the part of our ministers and teachers lest they should add to the spirit of unrest that comes of injustice and proscription. Wisdom dictates that by all means a conflict between the races should be avoided. The Europeans, armed and drilled, would have the advantage of all others, and there could be but one result. The Kingdom of God does not proceed in its conquests by the employment of carnal weapons, and right can afford to be patient because it is bound to win in the end.

The native people have had enough of war. Their vocation in the ages past was to war among themselves, and it would not be difficult to impress them that that is not the way to right their wrongs. But the new life which we offer them is the life of peace and good will, and they cannot believe in God and our holy religion without believing that He is able to carry out His purposes, tho He be long-suffering.

My stay in Africa was pleasant, for I did not count the deprivations, and sometimes hardships. We were graciously kept from disease, even the bubonic plague that came to our very door. I was permitted to go with my husband thru the greater portion of his work, and mingle with and talk to the women upon the subjects of righteousness, temperance and the judgment to come. If some seed was sown that took root, and will never be entirely uprooted, the visit to Africa was not in vain. In selecting names for our local auxiliary societies, we chose the names of some of the women at home who labored during their lifetime in home missions, besides helping the foreign work. And so we have the Mary A. Campbell Society at one place, the Florida Grant at another, and other names of worthy ones which will be handed down to posterity, and be a means of inspiring those who will be told of their work and worth.

PART II

———

Biographical Sketches of Teachers, Graduates and Undergraduates of the Institute For Colored Youth

———

Illustrated

W. C. BOLIVAR

INTRODUCTION TO PART SECOND

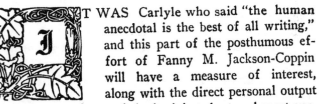

T WAS Carlyle who said "the human anecdotal is the best of all writing," and this part of the posthumous effort of Fanny M. Jackson-Coppin will have a measure of interest, along with the direct personal output from the pen of one of the brainiest, best and most useful women of Negro origin. For many years the writer urged with others some tangibility from her pen, and it was only after an enforced home keeping, through sickness, that it was at last undertaken. She "crossed the bar" in January and the autumn prior found the book practically finished. In several talks, including one, just five days previous to her final leavetaking, she was full of regret that the data accumulated by her had not taken the finished form of the first part. It was at hand, however, but not codified and arranged in sequence. The spirit of altruism, the self-abnegations of a lifetime, were obvious in her motive in the other part she had planned. She meant that those who had helped her, and that some of the exceptional scholars from the school in which she had taught for nearly forty years, should be a part of her last effort. All the details, and all the persons noted in the pages to follow, were her thought, suggestion, and arrangement. She is recalled by the writer from the time of her advent in Philadelphia, and all the way thru he has followed her career not only with profit and interest, but with admiration. He knows of the many needy, ambitious and purposeful boys and girls she helped, not only by suggestions, but practically. He is aware of the initial steps to combine both head and hand training, and how as far back as the Centennial days, which seemed to be the fulcrum for her lever, she started the project, that was seen in the trades that were taught along with academics. The managers had a practical demonstration of her belief in the way she secured several thousand dollars as an earnest of it. This was even before 1880, antedating Tuskegee, and a few years later the Managers were convinced, and the school set in motion with the money in hand. Two efforts of a tentative character, with the head and hand combination, were made with insufficient funds in the '30's, at Eddington and Chester County. There was then a halt, and the school was not started again until the '40's, and carried on for a brief span by Ishmael Locke. There was another closing of the school, but money came by bequest and gift, and the idea of mind training alone was set in motion, and continued under Professors Reason and Bassett and Mrs. Coppin herself, until the change came as narrated.

This is simply a supplementary pointer to an aftermath of splendid effort, as seen in the first part; and in no sense an introduction—for who is there to introduce a woman like Fanny M. Jackson-Coppin?

WILLIAM C. BOLIVAR.

INSTITUTE FOR COLORED YOUTH

BIOGRAPHICAL SKETCHES OF INSTITUTE TEACHERS, GRADUATES AND UNDER-GRADUATES

Charles L. Reason.—Ishmael Locke was the first teacher for the Institute for Colored Youth, and his tenure was brief, for the reason of insufficient funds. When this was secured, the managers put up the building at 716-18 Lombard street, and secured Prof. Charles L. Reason as its head. Prof. Reason was a native of New York city, and a graduate of the Mc-Grawville College, N. Y. In 1849 he was called to the chair of Belles Lettres and Mathematics, in New York Central College, and relinquished his work there to come to Philadelphia. He remained but two years, when he went to his native city and became principal of the largest public school there. He was a man of rare personality and finely equipped for teaching. He was cultured beyond most of his contemporaries, and wrote strongly and gracefully both verse and prose. In all the anti-slavery publications he was a contributor, as well as to the Anglo-African Magazine, begun in New York in 1859 under men like Dr. James McCune Smith. He lived to a ripe age, and not only in the educational field was he a potency, but in all the concerns of a public character in which his race was a

139

part. A singular coincidence was the fact of a call to Grace M. Mapps, of this city, as the head of the Girls' Department, I. C. Y., at the time of Professor Reason's call. She was a graduate of McGrawville College, and the pioneer colored woman as a college graduate.

Hon. **Ebenezer D. Bassett** was the principal in charge of the Institute for Colored Youth who immediately preceded Mrs. Fanny Jackson-Coppin.

Mr. Bassett was born in Litchfield, Connecticut, attended the Birmingham Academy, now known as the Derby High School, and was graduated from the Connecticut State Normal School at New Britain in 1853. He also studied at Yale in '54 and '55. It was in the fall of '55 that he accepted the position as principal of the Institute for Colored Youth. He remained here for fourteen years. He was an earnest, forceful teacher, always painstaking, always faithful to his duties, and was especially successful in the teaching of mathematics and the classics, in which he had excelled while a student at Yale.

In 1869 he was appointed first United States Minister to Haiti by President Grant, and served in this capacity until 1879.

Our government's appreciation of his services is shown in the acceptance of his manual on the "Resources and Government of Haiti" as authoritative by the Bureau of American Republics, at Washington.

During one of his visits to his home at New Haven

Prof. C. L. Reason   Hon. E. D. Bassett

Prof. Robt. Campbell   Martha F. Minton   Prof. Octavius V. Catto

Prof. Jacob C. White, Jr.   R. E. DeR. Venning

he was invited and delivered an address upon "The Right of Asylum," before the Law School at Yale.

On his return to the States the Haitien Government appointed him Consul General at New York city. This position he held for twelve years. Again in 1898, at the outbreak of the Spanish War, the people of Haiti, fearing that they might be included in the annexation which was then under discussion, desired the advantage of Mr. Bassett's experience and advice. He was then reappointed as Vice Consul. This position he held until his death, November 13, 1908.

It was during Mr. Bassett's administration as principal of the Institute that the first examination and appointment of colored teachers obtained in our public schools.

Octavius V. Catto was born in Charleston, S. C., February 22, 1840, but came to Philadelphia with his parents at an early age.

He attended the Institute for Colored Youth and graduated therefrom as the valedictorian of his class in 1858. He was immediately appointed assistant to the Principal, the late Hon. E. D. Bassett, as teacher of English and Mathematics.

In the early "sixties" he was called to the principalship of a Grammar School in Brooklyn, but, declining this offer, he remained assistant to Mr. Bassett until 1869, when the latter was appointed Minister to Haiti by President Grant. Mr. Catto then became Principal of the Boys' High School Department of the Institute.

The following year he was granted a month's leave of absence by the Board of Managers so that he might go to Washington, D. C., at the request of the school authorities there, to revise the course of instruction for the public schools of that city. This was done because he had declined the appointment of Superintendent of Colored Schools which they had tendered him, as the Managers of the Institute were equally desirous of retaining him here in Philadelphia.

He was one of the famous ninety colored men who answered the first call for troops in the North in the late Civil War, and who were turned away from the Capitol at Harrisburg by Governor Curtin, who declared no colored soldiers should cross the State of Pennsylvania while he was Governor.

He drafted the Bill of Rights for equal accommodation for all in the cars of our city, and was also one of the committee who repeatedly visited Harrisburg, accompanied by the late Prof. Jacob C. White, Jr., who for many years was Principal of the Roberts Vaux School, of the Fourteenth Section. Thru the persistent efforts of Mr. Catto and his committee the passage of the bill was secured, and it remains intact to-day.

Mr. Catto was one of the founders of the Banneker Institute, a literary association of considerable merit, which was in existence over twenty years. He was also an active member of the Philadelphia Library

Company, which had been organized in 1832 and was not disbanded until after his death.

He was a speaker of pleasing voice, gracious yet forceful manner and persuasive power. He was an upright, intelligent citizen, who took active part in all intellectual affairs of the hour.

His strong belief in the power of education in the development of a people is well shown in the following quotation from one of his addresses: "It is the duty of every man, to the extent of his interest and means, to provide for the immediate improvement of the four or five millions of ignorant and previously dependent laborers who will be thrown upon society in the reorganization of the Union. It is for the good of the nation that every element of its population be wisely instructed in the advantages of a republican government, that every element of its people, mingled tho they be, shall have a true and intelligent conception of the allegiance due to the established powers."

He was cruelly assassinated by a political enemy, on October 10, 1871, while returning to his home from school.

The city authorities accorded him as great honor as was ever given to any citizen, the city officials attending the funeral, which expenses were borne by the city government.

A just condemnation of the deed which caused his untimely end, no less than a just appreciation of his many manly and noble traits, led the Board of

School Directors of the Seventh Section, with the late Thomas Durham as president, to request the Board of Education to name the Public School on Lombard street, west of Twentieth street, in his honor, at its dedication in January, 1879.

Among the number of young people who were inspired by the late Fanny Jackson Coppin to take advantage of the opportunities offered for skilled hand training in the Industrial Department of the I. C. Y. were **Ida A. Burrell and Helen M. Burrell**, granddaughters of the late Jno. Pierre Burr, one of the prime movers in having the Humphrey Fund applied to the education of Negro Youth and thereby marking the beginning of the Institute for Colored Youth. Both of these young women have become examples of what industry, skill and close attention to business will do for any one who is steadfast and earnest in his purpose in life.

Pliny Ishmael Locke.—Born April 27, 1850, eldest son of Ishmael Locke, teacher and first principal of the school under the Humphrey bequest that eventually became the Institute for Colored Youth. Educated I. C. Y., graduated 1867. Taught in Tennessee under the Freedman's Bureau, '67-'68. Instructor at the I. C. Y., '68-'71, in mathematics and other branches. Appointed clerk Freedman's Bureau, Washington, '71-'72, first colored appointee under the civil service, clerkship second auditor's office, Treasury Department, Washington, '72-'76. Studied law at Howard University, LL. B., 1874. Principal colored school,

Hon. J. E. Lee   Hon. J. H. Smythe

Prof. Frazelia Campbell   Prof. E. A. Bouchet   Laura F. Barney

Hon. John S. Durham   William Adger

Chester, Pa., '79-'83. In '83 first colored appointee under the local civil service to clerkship money order department, Philadelphia Postoffice, '83-'86. Returned to principalship Chester school, '87-'90. Customs clerk, '90-'91, and '91-'92 clerk Department of Public Works, Philadelphia. Died August 23, 1892.

Henrietta R. Farrelly, 1876, is principal of the Pollock School and **William E. Cooper,** 1867, of the Wilmot School, in Philadelphia.

William H. F. Armstead was for many years head of the Camden, N. J., grammar school, and was later on succeeded by Malachi Cornish, who still holds the position.

Among the former pupils of the I. C. Y. to graduate from the U. of P. are: James T. Potter, George R. Hilton, Eugene T. Hinson, William H. Warrick, Conwell Banton, Hiram Williams.

William E. Augusta, Andrew F. Hill and John H. Smythe were three I. C. Y. graduates to serve as cashiers of banks under the Freedmen's Bureau.

Among the first principals and teachers in the schools at the National Capital, after grading, were; **Sarah L. Daffin,** Sarah Iredell, Laura Iredell, Maria C. Barney, Laura J. Barney, Lucretia Douglass, Narcissa George, Louisa P. Matthews and Martha N. Matthews.

Morris Layton, an alumnus, has been the head of the Harrisburg, Pa., grammar school for more than a quarter of a century.

10

Rebecca J. Cole, class of 1863, studied medicine at the Woman's Medical College, Philadelphia, and the first of the race from that institution.

Mary E. Lindsey, now Murdah, class of 1880, studied kindergarten and was the first teacher of that system in Philadelphia.

Caroline Still, now Anderson, an undergraduate of the I. C. Y., is a graduate of Oberlin College, Ohio, and afterward of the Women's Medical College, Philadelphia.

Martha Howard, of Fall River, Mass., was for several years an assistant to Sarah M. Douglass in the Girls' Preparatory Department.

Richard T. Greener, a native Philadelphian, graduated from Harvard University in 1869, and began to teach at the I. C. Y. in 1870. He was a well-equipped man and a clever writer. He went to South Carolina and became Dean of the Law School at the capital of that state. During the Russian-Japanese war he was consul at Vladivostok, and held his position through all of that contest. He is now practising law in Chicago.

W. H. Josephus was a native of B. W. I., a scholarly man and taught for several seasons in the I. C. Y. under Fanny M. Jackson.

Joseph E. Lee was born in Philadelphia and graduated in the class of 1869. The most of his active life has been spent in Florida, where he studied law, became a legal officer of the state, Collector of Internal Revenue and Collector of the Port. He is a man with remarkable ability, and has held important offices, both state and national, longer than any other colored person. He has acquired a considerable fortune.

Laura F. Barney, was born in Philadelphia. Her first schooling was in the Friends' School, Byberry, 23d ward. She entered the I. C. Y. and graduated in 1871. She taught at Chester, Pa., and then in Washington, D. C., finally becoming Assistant Superintendent of the High School there, where she had the finest rating. In the list of the premier teachers in the Washington, D. C., schools the following were from the I. C. Y.: Laura F. and Maria C. Barney, Sarah L. and Laura Iredell, Sarah L. Daffin, Narcissa George, Lucretia. M. Douglass, Louisa P. and Martha N. Matthews, Sarah L. Iredell taught in the I. C. Y. and in Vaux Public School, Philadelphia, and years after became head nurse at Freedmen's Hospital, Washington, D. C.

It is a noteworthy fact that **Theophilus J. Minton, John W. Cromwell, William J. Cole,** and **Pliny I. Locke,** all I. C. Y. graduates, held the highest grade departmental clerkships at the national capital, and John W. Cromwell is now Principal of a grammar school there.

Theophilus J. Minton graduated from the I. C. Y. in 1866. He represented Forney's Philadelphia Press in Virginia during the Reconstruction Period and then

gravitated to S. C. Here he took up the law and practised his profession, as well as holding public office.
Later on he went to Washington and entered the government service, and then to Philadelphia (his birth-
place), where he practised law until his death.

James F. Needham, a native of Philadelphia, who
graduated at 14; clerk, teacher at Chester
and the I. C. Y., and connected with the tax office as
clerk, discount officer and for a while Deputy Collector
of Taxes. Much of the present tax office system
evolved from and was shaped by him. Grand Master of
the Odd Fellows for two terms and now Grand Secretary. A wonderful mathematician, an excellent scholar
and a clever business man.

Richard E. DeR. Venning, born in Philadelphia,
graduated from I. C. Y., class 1867. Taught in Maryland, the I. C. Y., was engaged in business for a span
and afterward (1881) entered the government service
at Washington, D. C., where he still remains. He had
high rating as teacher of mental arithmetic.

Jeremiah Scott, a native of Philadelphia and class
1870. First colored man to be admitted to the Philadelphia courts as an attorney.

Sarah M. Douglass was one of the most unique
figures in the field of education. A native of this city,
and born over one hundred years ago, she was educated
by tutors, and began teaching directly after and continued that work for more than sixty years. She be-

REV. N. F. BROOKS   PLINEY I. LOCKE

JULIA F. JONES   PROF. J. E. HILL   CHARLOTTE BASSETT

·PROF. CHARLES A. DORSEY   PROF. HOWARD DAY

gan at the I. C. Y. in 1853 and continued on during the principalships of Professors Reason and Bassett and Fanny M. Jackson-Coppin. She adhered to the tenets of the Friends and always attended their meetings. Her whole course was as teacher in the Girls' Preparatory Department. She was a contributor to the early anti-slavery publications, and a lecturer of note.

Grace A. Mapps was the first among the women of her race to finish a college course at McGrawville, New York State. She came to the Institute for Colored Youth, along with Prof. Reason, and taught about twelve years, as head of the Girls' High School. She was a frequent contributor to several periodicals prior to the Civil War, and had a literary rating of a high order. She was a native of Burlington, N. J., and died there several years ago.

Martha A. Farbeaux, afterward **Minton,** was the first woman graduate of the Institute for Colored Youth, and taught there under Prof. Bassett until her marriage. Years after, she again taught during the principalship of Fanny M. Jackson-Coppin. She was an excellent teacher and endeared herself to all who came under her. She is still living, and the solitary link between the original school and today.

James M. Baxter, a native Philadelphian, graduated from the I. C. Y. in 1864, at eighteen. Directly after he received a call to Newark, N. J., to take charge of its only public school for colored children, and continued as its head for forty-six years. He developed the school, and it became a very large one, ranking with the best in that city. He not only made an impression as an educator, but was active in all the affairs of his adopted city, both secular and religious. Many of the scholars attained distinction, in business and the professions. He kept pace with all the modern systems of teaching and was rated by the educational authorities as a teacher of rare value.

Charles A. Dorsey, a native of Philadelphia; his first school life was at Birds School, now the James Forten, then at the I. C. Y., under Prof. Chas. L. Reason. He left and matriculated at Oberlin College, Ohio, graduating therefrom in 1863. He immediately accepted the Principalship of a large school in Brooklyn, and taught for more than forty-five years. He was before his career closed, school supervisor of Brooklyn. In all the affairs of his adopted city, religious, civil and political, he was a potent factor. He was a man of wide learning, a teacher of merit and a citizen of the best character. For a while he was a fellow-student of the author of this book.

William Adger, born in the city of Philadelphia, June 8, 1857. He received his early education at the I. C. Y., graduating with the brightest honors in 1875, after which he prepared himself for the University of Pennsylvania, entering the college department in 1879, and graduating with a B. A. degree in 1883. His college career was rather interesting from the fact of his being the first colored man to enter the University and the first colored man, up to that time, to graduate from the Academic Department with the B. A. degree.

The Faculty and students from the time of his entrance till his successful closing watched him with a degree of closeness that thoroughly enabled them to say of him, that by his scholarly and moral deportment he made it possible for the doors of the University of Pennsylvania to remain open to the members of his race. His moral and educational training prepared him to be one of the best equipped students to enter the Episcopal Seminary in the fall of 1883.

He was secretary to Mrs. Fanny J. Coppin for ten years. His short life ended October 10, 1885, during his senior year in the Seminary.

The Institute for Colored Youth has had its representatives in the different professions and activities of the District of Columbia for more than a generation. When colored clerks in the civil service were considerably fewer than today, it was only thru rigid examinations that colored men were appointed. Among the first were **John H. Smythe** and **James Le Count, Jr.,** in the census office. This was forty years ago. Next was **William J. Cole,** in the census office. Smythe's career was most remarkable. He became clerk in the Freedmen's Bank, an assistant cashier in Wilmington, N. C., then a member of the Constitutional Convention of that state. During the Hayes administration he went to Washington, resumed the practice of law, until his appointment as U. S. Minister to Liberia, which position, with only a brief interval, he filled until the election of President Cleveland, in 1885. Subsequently he went to Virginia, became active in the affairs of the True Reformers, was for a time its editor, and subsequently, as the crowning event of his life, he established the Negro Reformatory, the first of its kind in the South. **William J. Cole,** as clerk in the census, rose to a confidential position, frequently representing the office before Congressional Committees. **Theophilus J. Minton,** after holding the position of bookkeeper in the Treasurer's office of South Carolina, went to Washington and entered the U. S. Treasury Department, and as law clerk in the office of the Controller, wrote many of the opinions of that official. **Miss Laura J. Barney** became Assistant Principal in the M St. (academical) High School, and as such shaped the educational training of hundreds who became successful teachers in the public schools of the national capital. Among other graduates of the I. C. Y. may be named **Mrs. Sarah A. Fleetwood** and **Laura Hawkesworth. Mrs. Lucretia M. Kelley** is still a clerk in the land office of the Interior Department, after years of service as teacher and matron.

Mr. **Pliny I. Locke** and **R. E. De R. Venning,** both former instructors in the Institute for Colored Youth, also reflected credit on their alma mater in the civil

J. W. HARRIS   PROF. C. L. MOORE

LIZZIE L. BURRELL   MAGGIE AUGUSTINE JONES   ESTHER A. REESE

PROF. C. ROBT. THOMPSON   PROF. JAMES M. BAXTER

service at Washington, D. C., the last named for many years an examiner of pensions.

Mr. J. W. Cromwell, also of the same institution, was one of the first colored men in Washington to reach a high grade clerkship in the civil service, and that entirely by competitive examinations. For fourteen years he published "The People's Advocate" and was one of the organizers of the American Negro Academy, of which he is still the Corresponding Secretary. He is also principal of one of the grammar schools.

Mr. Charles N. Thomas was the first colored lawyer to practice before the courts of the District of Columbia, having been admitted with several others, graduates of the first law class from Howard University, in 1871. Before his phenomenal public career in Florida, **Joseph E. Lee** held a confidential clerkship to the late Alexander Shepherd, Governor of the District of Columbia.

Eugene R. Belcher, also a representative of the Institute, for many years prominent in the federal politics of Georgia, while in Washington was clerk in the Freedmen's Bureau, and was recognized as one of the very best classical and mathematical scholars "on the Hill," as Howard University was known, where he was eagerly sought by all perplexed students.

Of later Institute graduates, residents of Washington, D. C., was **Miss Lucy Addison.** Miss Addison, at Roanoke, Va., has done a monumental work as an educator, and her influence as such is recognized thruout southwest Virginia.

Fanny Ramsey Harris, Pennsylvanian by birth, graduate of the I. C. Y., in 1881, studied and taught kindergarten until 1883. Entered upon duty as teacher of kindergarten and elementary studies at the "House of Industry," Philadelphia, September, 1883, and remained until June, 1892. In September of the same year joined the corps of teachers at the I. C. Y. and continued there until its close, June, 1902. In August, 1902, was appointed assistant matron at the Home for Aged and Infirm Colored Persons, continued as such until October, 1904.

Helen Brooks Irvin, a graduate of the I. C. Y., is a member of the staff of teachers at Howard University, Washington, D. C.

Miss Frazelia Campbell is a graduate of the I. C. Y., class '67, and has taught continuously since. Specialized in Latin, German and Spanish. Has gained an enviable reputation as a teacher and as a woman with great strength of character.

When the Institute for Colored Youth discontinued its academic work and moved to the country to make a specialty of Normal and Industrial work, Miss Campbell accepted a call to Allen University, at Columbia, S. C., where she has taught with marked success, and where she now teaches.

Dr. Alice Woodby McKane, now a practicing physician in Boston, is one among many graduates of the

I. C. Y. who has had an active and interesting career. With her husband, she established a hospital at Savannah, Ga., and at Monrovia, west coast of Africa.

Edward Alexander Bouchet, born September 15th, 1852, at New Haven, Conn., prepared for college in New Haven High School and Hopkins Grammar School, New Haven. Entered Yale College, 1870. Graduated, A. B., 1874, and received the degree Ph. D. in 1876. Came to the Institute for Colored Youth September 1, 1876, and was teacher of chemistry and physics to June, 1902, a period of 26 years. Is at present Principal of Lincoln High School, at Gallipolis, Ohio.

Martha F. Minton graduated from the I. C. Y., 1858, was appointed assistant teacher in 1859 and taught until 1863. Afterwards taught at the "Bee Hive," also a "Friends' School," at Locust Street and Raspberry Alley, where the Joseph Sturge Sunday School was and is still held.

Returned again to the I. C. Y. as teacher of sewing and examiner of pupils for dressmaking classes in the Industrial Department of the school until she resigned.

Robert Campbell, a native of the British West Indies and a man deeply grounded in the sciences, came to the I. C. Y. just after the induction of Ebenezer D. Bassett as Principal. He taught for four years and then went to Africa at the expense and instance of the Colonization Society, and with the further object of research work. His investigations were wide reaching,

and set forth in two books, one of which, "My Mother-
land," attracted widespread attention. His tenure in
Africa covered several years, ending only with his
death. He had the gift of imparting, and while at the
Institute for Colored Youth endeared himself to its
scholars by reason of that and many other worthy attributes.

Jacob C. White, Jr., went from Bird's School to
the new Institute for Colored Youth when Prof.
Charles L. Reason became its head. He was its first
and solitary graduate and, before receiving his diploma,
organized and taught in the preparatory department.
He then became its full-fledged head and remained
until 1864, when he was elected Principal of the Robert Vaux Public School. He was its head until his
retirement in 1905, a period of forty-one years. Scores
of boys and girls passed from under his care, and the
general result of his training has been obvious in every
avenue of life in this city and elsewhere. When he
became a pensioner, the Board of Education passed
a series of resolutions of the most flattering character.
Not only was Mr. White noted as an educator, but
he was a force in all the general activities of his
native city, as founder of the Banneker Institute; in
the affairs of the Underground Railroad; the Social,
Civil and Statistical Association; first President of the
Board of Managers of the Frederick Douglass Me-
morial Hospital; the Equal Rights League; the State
Militia; one of the first ninety to offer service in the
War of the Rebellion in 1863; as correspondent of the

DR. ROBT. JONES ABELE   REV. CARLTON M. TANNER

FLORENCE LEWIS BENTLEY   JULIA SONGO WILLIAMS   FANNY RAMSEY HARRIS

PROF. MALACHI D. CORNISH   JAMES H. WILLIAMS

Anglo-African; Secretary of the Pythian Club; Elder in the First Presbyterian Church, and in scores of efforts for the betterment of his kind. He was not only the premiere graduate of the I. C. Y., but among the most distinguished pupils.

Jesse Ewing Glasgow left before his graduation and was given a certificate of proficiency by the Principal and Managers of the I. C. Y. He was well enough grounded in Greek, Latin, Philosophy and the higher mathematcs to matriculate at Glasgow University, Scotland, in 1856.

At this ancient seat of learning he pursued his studies for nearly four years and died before his graduation. He ranked high as a scholar, and while at the Scottish University excelled in both Mathematics and Literature. He came of Quaker City stock and was a blood relative of the eminent Henry Highland Garnet.

Frances E. Rollin Whipper was an undergraduate and left one year before the end of her course. She went to Charleston and taught school, just after the United States army had captured the city. She wrote the life of Major Martin R. Delaney, an ample work and in excellent style. She was a bright scholar, and besides the book just noted, contributed to the publications just at the close and after the Civil War. Her husband was a state senator in South Carolina and the nephew of William Whipper, of Pennsylvania.

W. F. Brooks, native of Philadelphia, Pa., a former teacher in the Institute for Colored Youth and a teacher of 24 years of experience. A Presbyterian minister. Degrees, A. B.; S. T. B.; and D. D. from Lincoln University, where he taught two years in the preparatory department and ten years in the I. C. Y. at Philadelphia. Taught as Principal of the Normal and Preparatory School of Biddle University.

C. Robert Thompson was born in New Brunswick, N. J., where he attended the public schools. Entered the I. C. Y. in 1891, from which school he graduated. Taught in the State of Delaware and at Somerville, N. J.

In 1900 he accepted the position of Principal of the Witherspoon Public School at Princeton, N. J., which position he now holds.

Thos. H. Murray, a native of Philadelphia, attended the Birds School, Philadelphia, now known as the James Forten Public School. A graduate of the I. C. Y. and attributes his success in life to the training he received at this school. He was the first colored person to receive a Principal's certificate to teach in the schools of Philadelphia. He is now teaching at Asbury Park, N. J.

John H. Smythe, LL. D., born 1844, in Richmond, Va. At the age of seven, Mr. Smythe was sent to Philadelphia to be educated. He attended private and public schools and graduated from the I. C. Y. in 1862. He was the first colored student admitted to the Academy of the Fine Arts in Philadelphia. He

joined the life class when 16 years of age. Later he
turned his attention to elocution. In 1862 he went
to England in an attempt to see Ira Aldridge, the colored tragedian, who at that time was in Russia. He
returned to America, studied law at Howard University, graduating in 1870. Was a clerk in the United
States Treasury at Washington. Later he moved
to Wilmington, N. C. From this State was sent as
Minister Resident and Consul General to Liberia,
West Africa. After 9 years of diplomatic service he
returned to America. In 1892 he accepted the editorship of "The Reformer," a Negro weekly published in
Richmond, Va. He soon became interested in the
youthful Negro delinquents of his State, and the crowning act of his life was the establishment of the Manual
Labor School of the Negro Reformatory Association
of Virginia.

Maggie Augustine-Jones.—When the Industrial
Department of the I. C. Y. was shaped and set in
motion by Fanny M. Jackson-Coppin, Maggie
Augustine was installed as teacher of cooking. She
organized this department, shaped and carried on its
work until her marriage to Ferdinand Jones. She
brought to this task splendid ability, and this was to
be expected from the granddaughter of Peter Augustine, the first man to introduce high art gastronomy
in this country, as far back as 1816. Our subject
settled in Mexico, where she died a few years ago.
Her school life, singular to say, was in New York,

under Chas L. Reason, the predecessor of E. D. Bassett.

Miles Tucker, class of 1876, entered University of Pennsylvania and won distinction in the Wharton School of that University as essayist and mathematician.

Harriett Johnson Loudin graduated in 1864 and taught in the Friends School, Wager Street, until called to the principalship of the Girls' Department, Allegheny, Pa.

John H. Anderson taught at the I. C. Y. in the early eighties. He was educated in New York State, and after a short tenure here, went West, and continued his profession.

Malachi Dunmore Cornish was born April 11, 1860 in Philadelphia, Pa. He is the son of David and Rachel Cornish. He attended the James Forten Grammar School (formerly the Bird School) and the Institute for Colored Youth, 9th and Bainbridge Sts., Philadelphia, Pa., graduating from the latter school in June, 1878.

He has taught in the following places: Nanticoke and Barren Creek Springs in Wicomico County, Md.; Merchantville, N. J.; Woodbury, N. J. He was also S. P. of the Colored Schools in the latter place. After remaining here five years, he resigned to take a position as Principal of the Gouldtown, N. J., public school. Four years later the Board of Education of the City of Camden, N. J., appointed him teacher of the

Thomas H. Murray

J. H. Anderson

Helen Burrell Smith

Ida Burrell Myers

Dr. I. Walter Sutton

Prof. Chas. H. Boyer

pupils in the West Jersey Orphanage. After a year he was made Principal of the Mt. Vernon Grammar School, Camden, N. J., which position he has held for the last fourteen years.

Henrietta Shepard Cornish, the wife of Malachi D. Cornish, was born in Philadelphia, Pa. She is the daughter of Jackson and Emily Shepard. She graduated from the I. C. Y., June, 1879.

She taught one year in Harford County, Md., four years in Glenolden, Pa. She was married August 26, 1884. A daughter was born May 15, 1885. In 1891, H. S. Cornish was appointed Principal of the North Woodbury School, which position she has filled for twenty-one years.

Andrew J. Jones, class of 1861, was for several years editor of the Philadelphia Sentinel.

Richard J. Warrick is one of the United States Civil Service examiners and secretary of the Board.

Elizabeth Ramsey, now Still, is a successful real estate dealer. She also taught for many years in the O. V. Catto Public School.

William W. Still is a lawyer. After leaving the I. C. Y., he entered Lincoln University, graduating therefrom.

Samuel J. Diton, after graduating from the I. C. Y., became a pupil of the Musical Department, University of Pennsylvania, and received the degree of Bachelor of Music.

11

Benjamin F. Sayre and R. J. Warrick, Jr., are dentists in successful practice.

Louise Parm is an instructor in the Baltimore High School.

Bertha T. Perry was for years business manager of *The Philadelphia Tribune.*

John Stephens Durham.—Born in Philadelphia, graduated from the Institute for Colored Youth in 1876. Was reporter on the *Philadelphia Press, Philadelphia Times,* editor of *"The Pennsylvanian"*—University of Pennsylvania; Assistant Editor of the *Evening Bulletin.* Taught school in Delaware. Clerk in Philadelphia Postoffice. Graduated from University of Pennsylvania, class ——. Read law and admitted to Philadelphia Bar. U. S. Consul to San Domingo. U. S. Minister to Haiti. Manager of a large sugar plantation in Cuba. Promoter of sugar interests on a large scale.

That Mr. Durham was given the Ministership to Haiti when he was quite a young man and with but little experience at that time in public affairs is an evidence of the fact that he is a man of unusual learning and strength of character.

Jackson B. Shepard, M. D., was born in Philadelphia, Pa., March 17, 1869. He is the son of Jackson and Emily Shepard. He attended the Primary School in the 8th Ward of Philadelphia, which was under the control of Quakers, and later on the Institute for Colored Youth, the Principal being Mrs. F. J. Coppin, from which he graduated in 1886.

In 1888 he taught school in St. Mary's County, Md. The following year, he was made one of the corps of teachers at the Christiansburg Institute, Christiansburg, Va. He also taught in Merchantville, Camden County, N. J.

During the next five years he was a clerk in the U. S. Pension Office, Washington, D. C. He graduated from the Medical Department of Howard University in 1894. He became Interne at Freedmen's Hospital. The next year and on July 1, 1895, was appointed by the Secretary of the Interior Department— First Assistant Surgeon at Freedmen's Hospital.

In August, 1896, he began the practice of medicine in Pittsburgh, Pa., where he still remains. He was married June 30, 1897, to Cora V. Smith, of Washington, D. C., the daughter of Richard and Elizabeth Smith.

William H. Polk, a native of Snow Hill, N. J., a graduate of the I. C. Y. class of 1886. Also a graduate of the Theological Department of Wilberforce University. His short and useful career ended after a few years' pastorate in the state of Ohio.

James Henry Williams, born October 23, 1864, Philadelphia, Pennsylvania. He received his earliest education in Quaker Schools, graduating from the Institute for Colored Youth in 1882.

He accepted the position of Assistant Principal of

the State Normal School at Sálisbury, N. C., term of 1882-1883. Having passed the Civil Service Examination, he entered the Postal Service in Philadelphia as a clerk in 1884. Two years later he was appointed Principal of a school in Elizabethtown, Kentucky, remaining for one term. Entered the annual examination, held at Louisville, Ky., for teachers in the public schools, was successful and received an appointment as teacher in the Grammar grade of one of the largest schools in that city. At the end of the term, Mr. Williams returned to Philadelphia and became a member of the firm, in the upholstery business, which had been established by his father, Carter Williams, in 1866, at Twelfth Street below Walnut Street.

Having finished a course at the Business College, and prepared himself in the knowledge of the trade, he became the active manager of the business. At the death of his father the firm became J. H. Williams & Co.

Julia I. Songow.—One of the well-known graduates of the I. C. Y. is Mrs. Julia I. Songow Williams, who immediately after her graduation was appointed as Principal of one of the Maryland schools— and by her earnest zeal and charming personality, was soon recognized as one of the most successful educators of her race. Her love for her alma mater encouraged a number of her pupils to finish their school course at the I. C. Y., some of whom are now ranked among the successful graduates.

In 1891 she received an appointment in the J. E.

HANNAH JONES BROWN

REV. W. H. POLK

DR ALICE WOODBY McKANE

GEORGE LOUIS SMILEY

JESSE EWING GLASGOW

Hill School, Philadelphia, and acted as Assistant to the Principal in the Day School and as Principal of the Night School.

In 1902 she married Mr. James H. Williams, a graduate of the I. C. Y. anu a prominent business man.

Mrs. Williams is a member of the Board of Managers of the Frederick Douglass Hospital, Vice President of the W. U. Day Nursery; Assistant Secretary of the Young Women's Christian Association and is active in many other charities.

P. Etienne Vidal, class of 1869, graduated from the University of Pennsylvania, Medical Department, and took post courses at Paris and Vienna.

Spencer P. Irvin has been Principal of a large school at Trenton, N. J., for more than thirty years, and is about to retire as a pensioner. He developed the system there, and his scholars have all made good in higher training.

Perry D. Robinson, M. D., is in lucrative practice of medicine in Lexington, Ky.

Joseph T. Seth, of the I. C. Y., is the owner of one of the largest undertaking establishments in Philadelphia.

Miss Annie Reeves, of the I. C. Y., holds a distinguished position as trained Nurse in the Public Schools of Philadelphia.

Carlton Miller Tanner was born in Philadelphia,

Pa., in the old building where the Christian Recorder was established and within one square of "Mother Bethel," the "cradle of African Methodism in America."

He is a graduate of the Institute for Colored Youth; of the Divinity School of the Protestant Episcopal Church in Philadelphia; a Doctor of Divinity of Wilberforce University, Payne Theological Seminary.

For twenty years he has been an active pastor and has held some of the largest charges in the A. M. E. Connection, now being the pastor of Big Bethel Church, Atlanta, Ga., with a membership of 2600 souls.

He was formerly secretary of the Tract Society of his Church; has traveled extensively thru the church in America, in the West Indies, and South Africa. In the latter field he remained for some time as a missionary. He established the *South African Christian Recorder* in 1902. He is the author of the "Probationer's Guide" and a "Manual of the A. M. E. Church," books adopted by the Church as text books for all applicants to enter the ministry of the A. M. E. Church.

Chas. L. Moore, born in the State of Virginia, February 3, 1861, attended school at his native home and in Philadelphia, at the House of Industry, Seventh and Catharine Streets. From this school he went to the Institute for Colored Youth, from which he graduated in 1881 as valedictorian and won the Latin prize of $15, which was given by the board of managers.

He taught in Maryland and in New Jersey. Was one of the organizers of the Maryland Colored State Teachers' Association, and of the "Educational Era," a paper printed during the school months in the interest of the colored pupils, schools and teachers of Maryland.

Returned to the I. C. Y. in September, 1892, as a teacher, which work he pursued successfully until the Institute was moved from the city.

Hannah Jones-Brown, wife of Rev. Howard D. Brown, is a native of Freehold, Monmouth County, N. J. She graduated from the Institute for Colored Youth during the principalship of the author, and taught for ten years at Freehold, N. J., her home town. She then accepted the position of principal of the Western District Colored School, 7th and Catharine Streets, Philadelphia, where she taught very acceptably for eighteen years, when she resigned to become the wife of Rev. H. D. Brown.

Chas. Henry Boyer, born at Elkton, Md., where he attended the public school and afterward went to the I. C. Y., Philadelphia, in September, 1881. Graduated in June, 1886. The salutatorian of his class. Taught four years in Maryland. In 1890 he went to New Haven, entered the Hopkins Grammar School to prepare for college. Graduated from Hopkins in '92, winning the prize for oratory. Entered Yale in

the fall, in the class of '96, with which class he graduated. Now has charge of St. Augustine College at
Raleigh, where he has given 17 years of valuable
service.

John W. Harris.—Another example of the energy
of the Philadelphia-born man is John W. Harris, a
real estate and insurance broker, of No. 1116 South
Nineteenth Street. Mr. Harris began his course of
education at the old Raspberry Street School and later
graduated from the Institute for Colored Youth (1886),
Immediately after the commencement, he entered the
office of *The Philadelphia Tribune* as clerk and performed his duties so well that he was in due time promoted to the managing editorship of the paper, at the
age of twenty-two.

For fourteen years he was connected with *The
Tribune,* during which time he engaged in the real
estate business, managing the Conservative Company,
in which he was very successful. *The Tribune,*
upon which he was formerly employed, speaks of him
as "hustling, reliable and painstaking in all of his
business transactions" and representing "the best
among our progressive young men."

Besides the home in which he lives, Mr. Harris
owns several other properties in this city. He is
Secretary of the Mercy Hospital and Training School
for Nurses, Treasurer of the Alumni Association of
the Institute for Colored Youth, a Director of the
Berean Building and Loan Association, Secretary of
the Donaldson Medicine Company, a Director of the

CHEMISTRY

CLASS IN CHEMISTRY

Concord Building and Loan Association, of which less than twelve per cent. of the stockholders are colored.

Mr. Geo. L. Smiley.—The subject of this sketch, Mr. George Louis Smiley, has the honor of being one of the youngest graduates of the Institute (having graduated at the precocious age of 15 years).

Immediately after graduation he became a clerk in one of the largest wholesale drug houses in this country, where he is still employed, having risen to a responsible position in the finance department of that concern.

Early in life Mr. Smiley became convinced of the expediency of versatility, hence did not confine his talents to one field, but delved into the art of photography; particularly excelling in the photography of horses and dogs. While yet a boy, he was invited to exhibit his photographs at the National Export Exposition. His exhibit there attracted marked attention and flattering comment. His pictures—entitled "The First Milking Lesson," and "The Little Pool" (illustrating one of Dunbar's poems)—at the close of the exposition were purchased by one of the leading magazines.

While on the subject of photography it would be well to note that the major part of the illustrations in this volume were made by this young man when he was 13 years old.

Another evidence of the versatility of this young man is found in his excellent elocutionary powers, which he has devoted to the rendition of Dunbar's poems, giving private recitals in the homes of some of the most exclusive millionaires. His rendition of Dunbar is "delightfully different"—Dunbar himself having said in the presence of the writer: "Young Smiley gets more of the subtle meaning out of my works than any other person I've heard. He has the rarest dialect and a fund of natural humor; never burlesques the race or resorts to facial grimaces, but makes you laugh with the race, not at them."

In addition to these widely different accomplishments, Mr. Smiley has achieved marked success as a writer of dialect stories; in fact his name might now be a household word, did he not modestly hide his identity under a "nom de plume."

I. Walter Sutton was born in the State of Louisiana and received his early education in Gilbert Industrial and Agricultural College.

He came to Philadelphia in the fall of 1890 and entered the I. C. Y., completing a course in carpentry in 1897 in that institution, and in 1898 graduated from the Academic Department.

September, 1898, he entered Hahnemann Homeopathic College Hospital of Philadelphia, graduating from that institution in 1903 and afterwards began the practice of medicine in Philadelphia.

Later in 1907 he returned to his alma mater and took a post-graduate course in Obstetrics; in 1907 was elected chief obstetrician of Mercy Hospital and Training School. He still retains the same position.

BRICKLAYING

CARPENTRY

He is a member of the County Homeopathic Medical Society and also a member of the Academy of Medicine and Allied Sciences.

Julia F. Jones, daughter of the late Robert Jones and Elizabeth Durham, is a native of Philadelphia, as were her parents. She is a lineal descendant of Absalom Jones, the founder of St. Thomas P. E. Church.

She was educated at the Institute for Colored Youth. Immediately after graduating Miss Jones assisted Sarah M. Douglas in the Preparatory Department of the Institute. She then took a position as principal of a public school in New Brunswick, N. J. There she remained ten years, demonstrating unusual ability as a wide-awake instructor and an excellent disciplinarian. She taught for two years in the State Normal School at Holly Springs, Mass., with marked success. At the end of this time, a vacancy occurring among the corps of teachers in the Institute, she was offered a position and urged to accept it. She returned to Philadelphia and was a highly honored member of the faculty until the closing of the Institute in Philadelphia. She specialized in botany, drawing and elocution.

The Civic Club of Philadelphia, an organization composed of some of Philadelphia's most intelligent and public-spirited women, nominated Miss Jones as school director of the Seventh ward.

Miss Jones has always been largely interested in benevolent work. She was president of the Women's

Union Missionary Society for a number of years, until that work was merged into the Women's Union Day Nursery. Miss Jones has been president of the Nursery ever since its establishment, in 1898.

Charlotte Bassett.—Miss Bassett was the daughter of the Hon. E. D. Bassett. She was a graduate of the Institute and began her career there as a teacher soon after graduation. Upon the closing of the Institute, in 1902, she was appointed an assistant in the Octavius V. Catto School.

With the passing of the Catto School, she was transferred to the Durham School. Here her efficient work led to her appointment as teacher in the grammar department.

On the ninth of December, 1912, Miss Bassett was suddenly called from her labors. Her death, so sudden and unexpected, was indeed a great shock to the community.

She was a woman of rare intellectual attainments, well versed as a linguist, especially in French, genial and amiable in manner, yet firm in controlling, kind and courteous to all. She was indeed the distinguished daughter of her distinguished father.

Her very presence was a benediction. She was in truth the most beloved of us all.

Requiescat in Pace.

Robert Jones Abele is a native of Philadelphia and a graduate of the Institute for Colored Youth, class of 1891. Directly after leaving the I. C. Y., he taught

PLAIN SEWING

DRESSMAKING

school at Belair, Maryland, for one year, and then matriculated at the Hahnemann Medical College, Philadelphia, where he finished the course in the distinguished list. He began the practice of medicine here at his home, and his ability at college was recognized by an appointment as one of the assistant surgeons at his Alma Mater, where he served as such for ten years. In the examination before the Pennsylvania State Board he obtained an average of ninety-seven and three-tenths, the highest known. From the beginning of the Mercy Hospital he has been on its staff. His practice is one of the largest and most lucrative in this city. He comes of a lineage that has been of great value to Philadelphia, one of his forbears being Absalom Jones, founder of the Protestant Episcopal Church among colored people in the United States, in 1792, as well as Clayton Durham, a co-worker with Richard Allen, in the organization of the A. M. E. Church Conference, in 1816.

Mrs. Sarah Maffett, teacher of Sewing and Dressmaking in the Girls' High and Normal School in Philadelphia, was appointed in the beginning to take charge of that work also in the Industrial Department of the I. C. Y. The teaching of so many classes was a great tax upon the strength of Mrs. Maffett, and she determined to give up some of them. She noticed that there was one pupil, who with some additional training, might be appointed as her successor. One of the requirements of the course was the drafting and making of a pattern at home. One day when the class was called upon to present patterns, one pupil found that her pattern was missing. She immediately asked the teacher to grant her a few minutes in which to make another, which she did, and won for herself the highest commendation.

This was the pupil that Mrs. Moffitt determined should be her successor. Mrs. Moffitt had the pupil apply herself at the school and after hours gave her further instructions in her own home to get the required course in less time.

After due consideration this pupil, Ida A. Burrell, was asked to assist Mrs. Moffit for a term of six months to demonstrate her ability to teach the work. At the expiration of this term of probation she was appointed to take charge of these classes, which she held until the close of the work of this school in Philadelphia. During this period of time she was called on to take charge of classes in sewing at the Hutchinson Street School for Colored Children and the classes formed during the existence of the Colored Women's Exchange and Dormitory for Girls, 754 South Twelfth St., managed and supervised by Mrs. F. J. Coppin.

Seeing the necessity for advancement, Miss Burrell took advanced work in New York City at S. T. Taylor's Establishment in Cutting and Designing. Special work at Drexel Institute in dressmaking. Knowing that the demand was for teachers in Manual Training who knew all branches of the work, Miss Burrell entered and completed the normal course in the Philadelphia Cooking School, and in September,

1906, received an appointment in Lincoln Institute, Jefferson City, Mo., to teach Domestic Science. She remained here one year, leaving to accept a position in the same work in the public schools in the city of St. Louis, Mo., where she taught four years, resigning to become the wife of J. W. Myers, instructor normal department, Sumner High School, of St. Louis, Mo.

Helen M. Burrell, by diligent application to work, attracted the attention of the teacher of Domestic Science (in the Industrial Department of the Institute for Colored Youth, Philadelphia, Pa.), Miss Imogene C. Belden. It was thru the influence of Miss Belden that the work of Miss H. Burrell was brought to the attention of Mrs. Sarah Tyson Rorer, principal of the Philadelphia Cooking School. When the course was completed, and during the annual exhibition of the work of the pupils of the I. C. Y., Mrs. Rorer visited the school, interviewed Mrs. Coppin concerning this pupil's work and personally invited Helen Burrell to take the normal course to prepare herself to teach the work. Being without funds to defray her expenses, Mrs. Rorer again came to the rescue and made it possible for her to work her way thru the school term by doing extra work before and after school hours.

When the Colored Women's Exchange and Dormitory for Girls was opened, on South Twelfth street, this young woman prepared and offered for sale preserved fruits, homemade candies, prepared by her own hands. It was thru the encouragement of Mrs.

Coppin that she was enabled to earn her first money in the practical work of preparing, cooking and serving a course dinner in honor of the birthday of one of the A. M. E. Bishops. Teaching seemed to be the profession that Miss Burrell was best fitted for, as she was successful in her season of teaching in the country schools of Maryland. She was called to take charge of the Domestic Science classes for colored girls when the Board of Education of the city of St. Louis decided to add manual training as part of the curriculum in that city. Here she taught successfully for over ten years, resigning her position to become the wife of Mr. Henry A. Smith, of the firm of Clark & Smith, Negro merchant tailors and haberdashers, in St. Louis, Mo., where she now resides.

William Oscar Davis graduated from the manual training department of the I. C. Y. (shoemaking department) in the class of 1893, and from the academic department, class 1894; was installed as a teacher in the Institute and taught during the years 1894-1897; went to Wilberforce in 1897 and studied theology at Payne Seminary, graduating with the degree of Bachelor of Divinity in 1900. After spending some time in the traveling ministry, entered Drew Theological Seminary at Madison, N. J, finished a three-years' course in two years, graduating with the class of 1904.

Besides successful ministerial work in the United States, he was pastor of the church at Hamilton, Bermuda, and Presiding Elder of the work on the Island

SWEEPING AND DUSTING

BED-MAKING

for four years. Returned to the United States, and is now pastoring at Wheeling, West Virginia.

Joseph E. Hill, who died on January 18, 1892, was a Philadelphian. His post-school training was under Miss Ada H. Hinton, followed by a short tenure at the Birds, but now James Forten School. Then he became a pupil at the Institute for Colored Youth, where he took the full course, graduating in 1873. He taught in Chester for awhile, and then became a part of the teaching staff of his alma mater, which only ended with his death. His work as teacher was indeed efficient, and it was a rule with him never to let a pupil go until he had grasped his lesson. He was not only faithful to his duties, but exceptionally conscientious. He never watched the clock, and only considered his school work ended when every task was finished. He took up expert accounting and bookkeeping, and received a diploma from one of our best business colleges. He was among the first students to matriculate at the Pennsylvania Academy of Industrial Arts, from which he graduated with honors. This equipment added to his duties at the Institute, and pretty soon the art course there became a feature. When Mrs. Fanny M. Jackson Coppin set in motion an industrial department, our subject assisted her. Not only in the detail work of its formation, but in all its movements afterwards. He was a man of engaging personality, and his whole career as teacher was a success. The moral sense in him was strong, and its effect on the

12

students of the Institute for Colored Youth was indeed pronounced. He was secretary of the Central Presbyterian Church Sunday-school, one of the founders and president, for eleven and a half years, of the Amphion Singing Society.

Mrs. Charles E. Bentley (born **Florence A. Lewis,** in Philadelphia,) entered the preparatory department of the I. C. Y. and finished the full course in 1876. She was an apt scholar and widely read, even as a girl. Directly after her graduation she took the teacher's examination for the public schools of her native city, and was appointed to a place in the Vaux School under Jacob C. White, Jr. She taught for many years, and then resigned to go into newspaper work. Her first place was with Golden Days, a children's paper, and then on the Times, under Colonel Alexander McClure, as a special writer. During the World's Fair at Chicago she was the correspondent of the Times. Coming home, she joined the staff of the Philadelphia Press, under Editor Charles Emory Smith, and remained with that paper until her marriage. She used the pen name of "Alice Irving," and ranked high as a clever writer in the journalistic field. For a while she was a contributor to the Chicago Times-Herald.

Theodore Gould, Jr., of the class of 1879, entered the University of Pennsylvania soon after, and duly graduated as an engineer four years later. He has pursued his profession in Boston quite successfully ever since.

Miss Esther A. Reese was born and reared in Philadelphia. She was graduated from the Institute for Colored Youth in the class of '85, taught a few years in the Industrial Department of said Institute. During these years Miss Reese had the care of an invalid and widowed mother.

While a scholar in the I. C. Y., Miss Reese showed such aptitude in art that, at the death of her mother, and through the kind patronage of her former preceptress, the late Mrs. Fanny J. Coppin, she entered and took the four years' teacher's course in the Penn Museum and School of Industrial Art. Then, not having the means at her command to pursue her art studies, again entered the schoolroom for teaching, this time in the City of Brooklyn as one of the five teachers in the Brooklyn Howard Colored Orphan Asylum, under the late Prof. Wm. F. Johnson, as superintendent, where she remained until the close of Doctor Johnson's career.

Since which time she has devoted more time to her specialty—art. She is now located in Philadelphia, giving both private and class lessons in drawing, painting, china painting and art-needlework. Miss Reese has given several very creditable exhibitions of her work in Philadelphia, Brooklyn and Asbury Park.

John Q. Allen was a teacher a part of the time of the incumbency of Mrs. Fanny M. Jackson-Coppin. He had a high rating for general scholarship, and resigned from the I. C. Y. to accept the principalship of a public school in Brooklyn.

Miss Matilda Baptiste, after graduating, engaged in business, and is associated with her sister in the largest catering trade in Philadelphia.

Mary Hawkins Locke. Graduate I. C. Y. 1869; teacher Chester school 1878-81; teacher Camden, N. J., 1881 to present date.

A private school organization conducted by **Cordelia A. Jennings,** a graduate of the Institute, was transferred to the public school system as an unclassified school, thru the untiring efforts of the Seventh School Section, of which the late Lewis Elkin was a member, and the donor of more than a million of dollars for the establishment of a fund for the retirement of teachers after twenty-five years of service.

When the Board of Education accepted the school, Miss Jennings was retained as principal.

So great was the increase of pupils that the services of three additional teachers were needed. It was at this time, September, '64, that the Board of Education decided to hold the first examination for teachers, which resulted in the appointment of **Caroline R. Le Count, Mary V. Brown** and **Mary H. Matthews.** Two were graduates of the Institute, of the classes of '63 and '64, and the other, an undergraduate of the class of '63.

This school was known as the Ohio Street Unclassified School.

In 1867 Miss Jennings was called to Louisville to take charge of a high school in that city. Another

CLASS IN COOKING

LIBRARY

examination was held in January of this year to fill the vacancy caused by Miss Jennings' resignation. As a result of this examination Miss Le Count was chosen principal.

A few years later, in 1878, the board decided to erect the building on Lombard street, west of Twentieth—the Octavius V. Cato School.

Since that time, until the closing of the building in December, 1910, the Institute furnished the greater number of the teachers, notably **Lucretia C. Miller, Elizabeth Ramsey Still, Annie E. Marriett, John S. Durham, John H. Clifton, Melinda J. Amos, Maria G. Jones, Dora Cole Lewis, Charlotte Bassett, M. Inez Cassey.**

Let it here be recorded to the credit of the Institute and teachers that at neither of these two examinations did any graduate or undergraduate fail to receive a certificate. Nor should this fact be omitted, that **Mrs. Mary F. Randolph, nee Durham,** former pupil of the O. V. Catto School, undergraduate of Institute and graduate of the Girls' High and Normal School; **Miss Annie E. Marriett** and **Miss Henrietta R. Farrelly,** graduates of the Institute, are the first to obtain certificates entitling them to hold positions as supervisors of the elementary schools.

In January, 1911, the Octavius V. Catto School was merged with two other schools of the district in the building located at Sixteenth and Lombard streets, as the Thomas Durham School. At this time Miss Miller and Miss Le Count retired from the profession.

SOME OF THE GRADUATES AND UNDER-
GRADUATES OF THE I. C. Y.

A.

Abele, Julian F.
Abele, Robert Jones
Accooe, Estelle
Adams, Cora
Addison, Elizabeth
Addison, Lucy
Adger, Anna P.
Adger, C. Samuel
Adger, Julian F.
Adger, Leon S.
Adger, Octavius (Mrs.)
Adger, Octavius V.
Adger, William
Allen, Emily
Allen, John Quincy
Alor, Rose
Alston, James F.
Alston, Mary Sampson
Amos, Malinda J.
Anderson, Anna Faun
Anderson, Caroline Still
Anderson, John H.
Anderson, Lena
Anderson, Mary
Armstead, Levi C.
Armstead, Lily C.

Armstead, William H. F.
Atwell, Cordelia Jennings
Augusta, Adolphus
Augusta, William E.
Augustine, Elizabeth B.
Ayers, Mary E.

B.

Bailey, S.
Baker, Henrietta
Banton, Conwell
Banton, Lydia M.
Baptiste, Henrietta
Baptiste, Matilda
Barber, Hattie Taylor
Barclay, Helen
Barney, Agnes
Barbour, Ida Bell
Barboza, Jennie
Barboza, Nettie
Barney, Emma
Barney, Laura F.
Barney, Maria
Bascom, Josephine D.
Bassett, Charlotte

Bassett, E. D., Jr.
Baxter, James M., Jr.
Baxter, Margaret
Bayard, Charlotte E.
Belcher, Eugene R.
Bell, William
Bently, Florence Lewis
Benton, Geo.
Berry, Bessie
Berry, Florence Massey
Berry, Linda Woodson
Billingsly, Caroline
Billingsly, Sarah S.
Blackson, James H.
Blick, Frederick
Boling, Edna W.
Boling, Fanny
Boling, Margaret Maston
Boling, Thomas H.
Bolivar, W. Carl
Booth, Nannie Bruff
Bowen, Idiana
Bowers, Alice C.
Boyer, Chas. H.
Boyer, Henry, Jr.
Boyer, Sarah P.
Braham, Hattie
Brice, Josephine B.
Brice, J. William
Brice, Oscar
Bright, Alexina O.
Bright, James
Brister, James
Brister, Olivia
Brooks, Essie

Broune, Celestine Lane
Brown, Clara
Brown, Elizabeth
Brown, Emma
Brown, Hannah Jones
Brown, Mary V.
Browne, Katie Collins
Browne, U. S.
Broxton, James
Bruce, Julia A.
Bunday, Mary
Burr, Emma
Burr, Letitia C.
Burr, Raymond J.
Burrell, Frank
Burrell, Helen M.
Burrell, Ida A.
Burrell, Lucinda
Burrell, Virginia L.
Burton, Chas.
Burton, Maria
Burton, Sophia
Bush, Blanche
Bush, John M.
Butler, John L.
Butler, Mary C.

C.

Campbell, Catherine S.
Campbell, Frazelia
Carr, Lucy
Carter, Ernestine LeCount
Carter, Katie

Carty, Ida
Cassey, M. Inez
Cassey, Mabel Price
Catto, Octavius V.
Certain, Daisy
Certain, James E.
Certain, Laurence
Chiles, Alex.
Clark, F. A.
Clark, James B.
Clayton, Robert Henry
Clifton, John H.
Cole, J. W.
Cole, Rebecca J.
Cole, William J.
Coleman, Camilla D.
Coleman, Ella
Coleman, Sylvester
Comegys, John W.
Comes, Silace
Comfort, Samuel
Conner, Theo. E. H.
Cooke, Elizabeth Abele
Cooke, Mary Abele
Cooper, Clarence
Cooper, H. H.
Cooper, Ida
Cooper, Mary B.
Cooper, Oscar
Cooper, Theodore
Cooper, W. H.
Cornish, Henrietta Shepherd
Cornish, Malachi D
Couzzins, Dandridge
Couzzins, Esther

Couzzins, Florence
Crawford, Mary
Creecy, Ulisses
Crippin, Andrew
Cromwell, John W.
Cropper, Alfred
Crosby, Florence
Curtis, R. L.
Curtis, Susan V.

D.

Daffin, Sarah L.
Daker, Celestine Truitt
Davenport, Garnetta
Davidson, Amaza
Davis, Estella
Davis, James D.
Davis, John H.
Davis, Laura
Davis, Mary
Davis, Mattie B.
Davis, Matilda
Davis, W. O.
Day, Dora White
Day, Howard
Delaney, Laura
De Munn, Karleen
Diety, Anna M.
Dingle, Ellis Y.
Dishroon, Matilda
Diton, Carl R.
Diton, S. J.
Dorsey, Charles A.
Dorsey, William

LAUNDRY

L'AUNDRY WORK

Dover, Mary Browne
Dowling, Laura
Duncan, Perry
Dunmore, Emma B.
Dunmore, William
Durham, John S.

E.

Edwards, Charles
Edwards, Henrietta V.
Eliricke, Priscilla E.
Elsey, Anyalette C.
Ennis, Laura
Evans, Chas. E.
Evans, Edward Clark
Evans, Julia
Evans, Olivia
Evans, Samuel B.

F.

Farrelly, Henrietta R.
Fells, Anna
Fields, Maria
Fisher, David
Fisher, John
Forbes, Ardena Lindsey
Ford, Fielding
Ford, J. W.
Francis, Jennie
Francis, William
Freeman, Chas.
Freeman, Elizabeth White
Freeman, Robins
Freeman, William

Frisby, Chas.
Frisby, Louisa
Frisby, Maecelina
Frisby, Sarah

G.

Games, William
Gantt, Mary
Gilbert, Adelaide F.
Gipon, Charles
Glasgow, Jesse E., Jr.
Goldsborough, Ida
Gould, Samuel G.
Gould, Theodore
Gray, Alice
Gray, Clara
Green, Olive
Green, Ottawa
Groves, William E.
Gumby, Eliza

H.

Hall, E. C.
Hall, Joseph
Hall, Katie
Handy, Elizabeth
Hargraves, Hannah Adger
Harris, Anna B.
Harris, Fanny Ramsey
Harris, Helen
Harris, James
Harris, John W.
Hart, Mary
Hawkins, Benjamin

Hawkins, Bessie
Hawkins, Evelyn
Hawkins, Julia Campbell
Hawkins, Mattie
Hayer, John
Hendricks, Laura Highgate
Henry, Bessie Mason
Henry, Sarah Richardson
Hewlett, Ralph
Highgate, Virginia
Hill, Andrew F.
Hill, Edwin
Hill, Elizabeth D.
Hill, Eva
Hill, Jennie
Hill, Joseph E.
Hilton, Geo. R.
Hinson, Eugene T.
Holden, Jesse
Holland, Lily
Holley, Louise
Hollis, William J.
Houston, Gertrude
Howard, M. E.
Howard, Randall
Howell, Andrew
Howell, Rush

I.

Iredell, Laura
Iredell, Sarah
Ireland, Annetta
Ireland, Helen
Irvin, Anna Jones
Irvin, Helen Brooks

Irvin, Ida Jones
Irvin, Spencer P.

J.

Jackson, Amanda
Jackson, Gertrude
Jackson, Howard
Jackson, J. Howard
Jackson, Lillian T.
Jackson, Mary Curtis
Jackson, Rachel A.
Jacobs, Florence
Jefferson, Fanny
Jeffreys, Mary E.
Jenkins, A.
Johnson, Anna
Johnson, Estellena
Johnson, Eva Price
Johnson, Harriett C.
Johnson, Ida
Johnson, James
Jones, Abram
Jones, Andrew J.
Jones, Celestine T.
Jones, Cecelia
Jones, David B.
Jones, F. J. R.
Jones, George
Jones, John D.
Jones, Julia F.
Jones, Maria G.
Jones, Rachel M.
Jones, Robert C.
Jones, Sarah E.

Jones, Thomas H.
Jones, William T.
Jones, W. H. R.
Jordan, Annie
Jordan, Gardine

K.

Kamp, Fanny
Kelly, Lucretia Douglass
King, Effie Palmer

L.

Lattimore, Andrew
Layton, Morris
Lawrence, Osceolo
Laws, Harry
Le Count, Caroline R.
Le Count, Corrine
Le Count, James, Jr.
Lee, Carrie
Lee, Joseph E.
Lee, Dora Needham
Leftwich, Emma
Lewis, Dora Cole
Lewis, James
Lewis, Sarah Masten
Lingham, Charles
Locke, Pliny I.
Locke, Mary Hawkins
Loper, Mary
Lowber, Harry H.
Lowber, Tillie Wells
Lowber, Wilbur W.

M.

Magrudar, Lotta
Marlowe, Mabel
Marriott, Annie E.
Marshall, Charles
Marshall, Cordelia
Mason, Florence
Massey, Clarence
Matthews, Louisa P.
Matthews, Martha N.
Merchant, Ida
Merrill, C. Price
Middletown, Albert
Milburn, Carrie
Miles, James T.
Miller, Annie
Miller, Eugenia
Miller, Lucretia C.
Mintus, Clara S.
Minton, Joseph
Minton, Martha F.
Minton, Mary F.
Minton, Theophlis
Minton, Virginia
Minton, William H.
Mitchell, Mabel
Mitchell, Mary
Morgan, Isaac
Morgan, James H.
Morgan, Rose F.
Moore, Charles
Moore, Charles L.
Moore, G. O.
Moore, Mary
Morris, Edward

Morris, Fannie C.
Morris, J. B.
Morris, Kate C.
Morris, William
Murdah, James
Murdah, Mary Lindsay
Murray, Abram
Murray, Elvira B.
Murray, Fanny
Murray, Thomas H.
Musserone, Etta C.
McDougald, Emma C.
McKane, Alice Woodby
McKenny, Augusta

N.

Needham, Dora B.
Needham, James F.
Neil, David A.
Neil, R. H.
Nichols, Gertrude S.
Nichols, Mary
Nichols, Sarah
Nicken, Lumberd L.
Nugent, Narcissa George

O.

Oberton, Clara
Offord, Wm. O.
Offitt, Gertrude M.
Owens, Bertha
Owens, Delaphine
Owens, Horace

P.

Page, Walter B.
Parker, Alice
Parker, Annie Godwin
Parker, Edith
Parker, Florence
Parker, Frank
Parker, Olivia C.
Parm, Louise
Parker, Theodore
Payne, Geo. E.
Philips, Sallie Cole
Pierce, Gertrude Freeman
Pierce, Janie Miller
Pitts, Marcus F.
Polk, Cyrus
Polk, Mary
Polk, Wm. H.
Potter, G. W.
Poulson, William A.
Powell, Janie Shepherd
Preston, Gertrude
Prettyman, Annie
Price, Corrine E.
Price, Jerome
Price, W. H.
Primas, Effie Ross
Pryor, Bertha T.
Purnell, John

R.

Ramsey, Emma
Ramsey, Samuel B.
Randolph, Lavina

GIRLS' ASSEMBLY ROOM

BASE-BALL TEAM

Randolph, Mary D.
Rawson, Arneta
Ray, Blanche
Reed, Esther
Reed, Katie
Reeves, Annie
Rice, Augusta
Rice, Janie Brice
Richards, Bertie
Richardson, Abbie
Richardson, Ella
Richardson, Fanny
Riddick, Izie
Riley, Agnes
Roberts, Geo. B., Jr.
Robins, Anna
Robins, Gertrude
Robinson, Annie
Robinson, George
Robinson, Gertrude
Robinson, Mary Campbell
Robinson, Perry D.
Robinson, William
Robinson, W. H.
Robinson, Virgie
Rogers, James
Rogers, Joseph H.
Roy, Howard
Royal, Georgie
Rumsey, Carrie Gould
Russell, Mary

S.

Sadlar, Clara
Salisbury, Novilla

Savage, Mary Dover
Sawyer, Perry
Sayers, Benjamin F.
Sayers, Esther
Selby, James
Seth, Alice B.
Seth, Felecia Ramsey
Seth, Henrietta D.
Seth, Joseph T.
Scott, Alexina
Scott, Charlotte E.
Scott, Elizabeth Mosley
Scott, Jeremiah
Scott, Malvina Gurley
Scott, Mary
Sharper, Mary
Sharper, Laura
Shepherd, Charlotte
Shepherd, Jackson B.
Shepherd, James
Shepherd, Lily
Showell, G.
Simmons, Elizabeth
Simmon, William
Sipple, Alverda
Smallwood, Hagar Ross
Smallwood, James L.
Smiley, C.
Smiley, Geo. L.
Smiley, Lily
Smith, Ethel
Smith, Florence
Smith, John H.
Smith, Mary

Smith, Mary
Smith, Nancy C.
Smith, Priscilla
Smythe, John H.
Snowden, Mary
Sparrow, Ophelia
Spence, Mary
Statts, Grace
Steeman, Drucilla
Stensin, Julia Bampfield
Stevens, Elizabeth B.
Stevens, Felicia E.
Stevens, Sarah A.
Stevenson, Sumner
Stewart, Josephine Leonard
Still, Ella Frances
Still, Elizabeth Ramsey
Still, Ephraim
Still, Fred
Still, Mary Potter
Still, William W.
Stokes, Ada Le Count
Sturges, D.
Sulliman, Hettie
Sumby, Elbert A.
Sutton, Charlotte Elligood
Sutton, I. Walter

T.

Tanner, Carlton M.
Tatam, Julia Alston
Taylor, Charles
Taylor, Clinton
Taylor, Emily

Thomas, Emma
Thomas, Mary
Thomas, Mary Needham
Thomas, Samuel
Thomas, William
Thompson, Chas. R.
Thompson, Maggie Smithers
Thompkins, Reba
Titus, Ella Marriott
Tolston, Ossula
Trulear, Eva George
Trulear, Maud
Trulear, Orita
Tucker, Jane
Tucker, Miles
Tucker, Nellie

V.

Venning, Miranda
Venning, R. E. De Reffe
Vidal, P. Etienne
Vodrey, Selena Hall

W.

Walker, Daisy
Walker, Gertrude
Walton, Rebecca
Walton, Mary
Waples, Ralph
Waples, William
Warrick, Fred
Warrick, R. J., Jr.
Warrick, R. J., Sr.

Warrick, Margaret
Ward, Frederick
Ward, Mary
Warfield, James A.
Warrick, Norris
Warrick, Virginia Bolivar
Warrick, William H.
Warwick, Julia Venning
Washington, Samuel
Washington, William
Webster, Thomas H.
West, Laura
Whales, Rosa
Whaley, Charles
Wheeler, Hattie
White, Annie
White, Jacob C., Jr.
White, Joseph S.
White, Martin M.
White, Maud
Williams, Chas.
Williams, David
Williams, Hiram
Williams, James H.
Williams, John H.

Williams, Julia Songo
Williams, Lee
Williams, Mary
Williams, Mary C
Williams, Rosetta
Williams, S. J.
Wilson, Annie
Wilson, Bella
Wilson, Charles I.
Wilson, Evelyn
Wilson, Gertrude
Wilson, Missie
Wilson, Morris H.
Woods, Franklin
Wood, Herbert B.
Woodlyn, Joshua
Wooten, Bessie Lowe
Wright, Robert
Wye, Geo.

Y.

Young, Clara
Young, Florence

ABOUT THE EDITORS

Henry Louis Gates, Jr., is the W. E. B. Du Bois Professor of the Humanities, Chair of the Afro-American Studies Department, and Director of the W. E. B. Du Bois Institute for Afro-American Research at Harvard University. One of the leading scholars of African-American literature and culture, he is the author of *Figures in Black: Words, Signs, and the Racial Self* (1987), *The Signifying Monkey: A Theory of Afro-American Literary Criticism* (1988), *Loose Canons: Notes on the Culture Wars* (1992), and the memoir *Colored People* (1994).

Jennifer Burton is in the Ph.D. program in English Language and Literature at Harvard University. She is the volume editor of *The Prize Plays and Other One-Acts* in this series. She was a contributor to *Great Lives from History: American Women*, and, with her mother and sister, coauthored two one-act plays, *Rita's Haircut* and *Litany of the Clothes*. Her creative non-fiction has appeared in *There and Back* and *Buffalo*, the Sunday magazine of the *Buffalo News*.

Shelley P. Haley is Associate Professor of Classics and Women's Studies at Hamilton College. Her writings on classical studies have appeared in *Historia*, *Classical World*, and *Classical Bulletin*, and she has lectured widely on early African-American women classicists and feminism in classical studies.